Catholic Perspectives on Reform

Michael Seewald

Paulist Press
New York / Mahwah, NJ

Cover design by Joe Gallagher
Book design by Lynn Else

Originally published in German as Michael Seewald, *Reform—Dieselbe Kirche anders denken* © 2019 Verlag Herder GmbH, Freiburg im Breisgau

Translated by Peter Dahm Robertson. English translation copyright © 2022 by Paulist Press, Inc.

Library of Congress Cataloging-in-Publication Data
Names: Seewald, Michael, 1987– author.
Title: Catholic perspectives on reform / Michael Seewald.
Description: New York / Mahwah, NJ : Paulist Press, [2022] | Includes bibliographical references. | Summary: "Reform is not "retrospective," but "future-oriented." The author argues that the Church's fundamental task is to "constantly rejuvenate the Gospel," to be a witness to God's workings in and through Jesus"—Provided by publisher.
Identifiers: LCCN 2022019062 (print) | LCCN 2022019063 (ebook) | ISBN 9780809155637 (paperback) | ISBN 9781587689611 (ebook)
Subjects: LCSH: Church renewal—Catholic Church.
Classification: LCC BX1746 .S383 2022 (print) | LCC BX1746 (ebook) | DDC 262/.02—dc23/eng/20220801
LC record available at https://lccn.loc.gov/2022019062
LC ebook record available at https://lccn.loc.gov/2022019063

ISBN 978-0-8091-5563-7 (paperback)
ISBN 978-1-58768-961-1 (e-book)

Published by Paulist Press
997 Macarthur Boulevard
Mahwah, New Jersey 07430
www.paulistpress.com

Printed and bound in the
United States of America

CONTENTS

INTRODUCTION

A Warning against "Bad Comedies"

Today's understanding of religion owes much to the Enlightenment, but today we remember its actual theological profile mostly in the form of key words. The Enlightenment was an attempt to unite two tendencies. On the one hand its theoretical complexity made it the exclusive project of a small segment of educated men and women. On the other hand, particularly in the late eighteenth century and especially in ecclesiastical circles, the Enlightenment tried to present its thinking in ways that were as simple as possible, practically popular. (This latter effort would be what earned the Enlightenment a reputation for superficiality in the eyes of Romantic thinkers.)[1] These two Enlightenment impulses—appreciation of both sophisticated thinking and its communication in simple words—are epitomized in Catholic theology by the work of Johann Michael Sailer.

Sailer developed what he called a *Theory of Reason for People as They Are*. In the vein of Kant, who was convinced that "in regard to the essential ends of human nature the highest philosophy cannot advance further than is possible under the guidance

which nature has bestowed even upon the most ordinary understanding,"[2] Sailer attempted to take up popular prescientific atti-
tudes and criticize them in such a way as to derive from them
precepts for rational behavior. Using questions that, not unlike a
manual of confession, seek to probe the reader's conscience, he
addresses several groups: teachers, writers, and reformers. He
tells this last group to reflect: "Will my reform not share the fate
of bad comedies, in which the author and the player share the
take, and the cheated public goes home unsatisfied?"[3] For a book
that invokes reform in its title, the metaphor in this question is
worth considering.

1. The word *reform* sounds attractive. Nowadays, with
   reforms being discussed everywhere, those who
   advertise themselves as reformers might no longer
   command the attention that a group of traveling
   actors received in Sailer's time. But in a Church that
   is desperately seeking something new without giving
   up any of the old, they will probably find interested
   listeners.

2. Mere interest is not enough to make reforms happen. Comedies, as the lighter form of theater, have
   an unearned reputation for being superficial. But
   a sophisticated comedy requires a skilled director
   who both feels a duty to the given text and also keeps
   a watchful eye on the audience to whom the text
   is supposed to mean something. In the same way,
   spreading the gospel requires reconciling those two
   aspects. And while the gospel should perhaps not be
   staged as a comedy, if it is to be the good news it
   claims, it should not be a tragedy, either.

3. All those who advocate reforms leave themselves open
   to attack, as evidenced by Sailer himself, who became
   bishop of Ratisbon (Regensburg) near the end of his
   life and suffered even posthumously from the vitu-
   peration one of his successors would raise against

him in Church politics.[4] While boring comedies or bad acting may be booed publicly, so that everyone knows where they stand, the Catholic Church has a hidden but by no means more civilized form of "quality control." Rumor has it that all too recently the Roman curia was egged on by a German bishop (no doubt intent on staging reform beyond his own see) to reintroduce the old tradition of the *index librorum prohibitorum* and to ban the publishing of books it deemed unsound. Authors, who are guaranteed the freedom to research by their respective national constitutions, remain uncowed. Nevertheless, the totalitarian and clandestine "theater critics" seeking to impose their notions of dogmatic good taste onto the stages of the world are up to their same old tricks only because the public does not know what abuses of power are being perpetrated in its name. (It might, however, be informed of these abuses at any time.)

4. Not everything labeled "reform" actually lives up to that name. Some loudly trumpeted reforms become mired in details and have no effect. Worse, others have an adverse effect, increasing the problems they claim to solve. To quote Sailer, reforms may fail because they merely rearrange the deck chairs; or they may fail because they seek to replace "the stolid village huts" that are dilapidated but at least still offer some shelter with "heavy, expensive palaces— built on sand."[5] It is therefore crucial to accurately assess the frame of possibility in which reforms can occur. That frame must be neither of utopian vastness nor of unimaginative smallness. The goal of this book—which is nothing more than an essay grown too long—is to precisely assess this frame.

This book aims to explore the *space of possibility* for reforms within the Catholic Church. To prevent misunderstandings from the very beginning: this is not a practical book and contains no laundry list of things to change. That does not mean that I have no opinion on the urgent questions of today—quite the contrary. I take stances on these questions elsewhere in my writings and lectures. But here I am concerned with another topic. The discourse on reform within the Church moves within a magisterially defined dogmatic framework that sets itself up as the only tenable form of Catholicism. But this framework is only one historically developed form of the Catholic faith, not the only possible one. To recognize this, one must be willing to place one's own theological position in historical context—or at least try, since one can never fully succeed. One remains an inextricable part of the history one is trying to interpret. But discourses with a magisterial (and thus authoritarian) bent are "generally not amenable to the radical nature of thorough (self-)historicization, because if taken seriously the process of historicization confronts one with the inescapable relativity of the own 'point of view.'"[6] Lately, such relativity of viewpoints must be discussed when a point of view has entered a crisis and is barely able to reveal the topic that it is meant to tackle. The question to ask then is, Can one look at this topic differently? Can one develop a new conception of the same Church?

To answer this question, we must first examine the magisterium's view of itself. Its statements generally make every effort to present the magisterium as the preserver and protector what is old and therefore true. But this is nothing other than historical politics, that is, the justification of structures of order using an interpretation of history that might well be interpreted differently. As the second chapter of this essay will show, the Church magisterium owes its current structure—which is young and still in the process of taking shape—to strategic attempts at modernization. Only by understanding the specific modernity of the magisterium can one perceive the immense effort of innovation the magisterium undertakes in order to seem as though all it wants is to preserve the old. This effort, and by extension this notion of modernity, explains why the magisterium has such difficulty with explicitly new ideas that arise from corrections of (apparently) old ones. The third chapter therefore distinguishes between three modes of dogmatic development: the mode of explicit self-correction (a rare phenomenon), the mode of "obliviscation" (an attempt to correct former teaching through targeted forgetting), and the mode of innovation veiling (a presentation of new ideas as old ones so as to create an impression of doctrinal continuity). The fourth chapter attempts a systematic and theological outline of the term *reform*, largely by determining the relationship between gospel and dogma. A final outlook completes the essay.

2

DOGMA AND ITS PROTECTIONS

Two Children of Modernity

THE MAGISTERIAL ARCHITECTURE OF THE CHURCH I

Walter Kasper has stated that "Church teaching and dogmatic teaching are *not* identical."[1] This statement is as self-evident as it is perplexing: What does it mean? Clearly, they cannot be two different teachings. There is not the set of Church teachings on the one hand, and on the other a separate set of dogmatic teachings. But it is also an insufficient description of their relationship to categorize dogmatic teaching as a mere subset of Church teaching—as if some parts of what the Church teaches were (already) and other parts were not (yet) dogma, while dogmatic teaching subsumes increasing parts of Church teaching until dogmatic teaching encompasses all of Church teaching. Instead, it makes more sense to see dogmatic teaching as a specific form into which Church teaching can be put.

It is characteristic of this dogmatic form of teaching that it results from a decision-making process. In the modern era, two features have been ascribed to that process: in the first place a judgment, or juridical ruling of the Church in the form of an authoritative *propositio*, must be presented. Second, this *propositio* must lay claim to a correct interpretation of the factual content of revelation. Only if these two conditions are fulfilled can Church teaching take on dogmatic form. The First Vatican Council, in *Dei Filius*, thus defines as follows: "Further, all those things are to be believed with divine and Catholic faith which are contained in the Word of God, written or handed down, and which the Church, either by a solemn judgment, or by her ordinary and universal magisterium, proposes for belief as having been divinely revealed."[2]

Those who think that the dogmatic form of teaching is limited to some few infallible ex cathedra papal rulings that constitute proper dogma are ignoring not only the full scope of Vatican I, but especially the subsequent "creeping infallibilization"[3] of Church teaching that continues to this day. Instead, Vatican I named two subjects capable of uttering dogmatically binding teachings in two ways: the pope and the entirety of the bishops—the Second Vatican Council would later use the term *college*.[4] Both of these subjects are invested with both the ordinary and extraordinary magisterium, that is, capable of issuing both ordinary and extraordinary teaching.

The bishops exercise this collegial power of the extraordinary magisterium through an ecumenical council, which—in the form of a general council of the Catholic Church under the leadership of the pope—makes the claim to represent ex parte the entire Church and to issue teachings that are binding for the entire Church.[5] The pope exercises his own extraordinary magisterium through papal primacy, that is, when he issues rulings ex cathedra "in discharge of the office of pastor and doctor of all Christians, by virtue of his supreme Apostolic authority."[6] The ordinary magisterium of the bishops is exercised collegially when the bishops across the world teach, in collective agreement and once again ex parte for the entire Church, a particular doctrine even without explicitly convening a council. The head of such an unconvened college remains the pope, and without him it cannot act. If, in his role as head of such a college, the pope determines a global consensus among the bishops, the content of the doctrine is considered definitively ruled and infallibly certain according to the self-definition of the magisterium.[7]

Whereas the extraordinary magisterium, regardless of the subject exercising it, and the ordinary magisterium as exercised by the college of bishops, both have a claim to infallibility, the ordinary magisterium as exercised by the pope alone, through primacy, represents a borderline case. The infallibility of the rulings of the papal ordinary magisterium is not set down in current magisterial precepts. But following Vatican I, the ordinary magisterium of the papacy, such as exercised in the encyclicals, has increasingly assumed the aura of the infallible.

For example, in his study on the ordinary magisterium—a study influential primarily in the Romance language world—Jean-Michel-Alfred Vacant advocated distinguishing between two kinds of ex cathedra rulings: those "presented through solemn decrees" and thus part of the pope's extraordinary magisterium, "and those presented by the ordinary, every-day magisterium of the sovereign pontiff," which as ex cathedra rulings were likewise liable to a claim of infallibility.[8] This maximalist interpretation of Vatican I hardly does justice to the Council as a whole, but can nevertheless marshal some specific phraseology in its support. For example, the Council demands an *actus fidei divinae et catholicae*, "highest most faithful assent," for teachings of both the extraordinary and ordinary magisterium (see *Dei Filius*). Since the text of the Council does not specify the subject of the latter, it implicitly includes the ordinary magisterium exercised by papal primacy.

The so-called encyclical paragraph in Pius XII's *Humani Generis* of 1950 shows how fond popes were of the idea that they might be able to issue definitive rulings and end debates even without a solemn exercise of their full sovereignty. The paragraph states that even when popes are not explicitly making use of the *suprema potestas* of their magisterium, Jesus's words in Luke nevertheless apply: "Whoever listens to you listens to me" (Luke 10:16). On principle, therefore, it is Christ himself who is speaking through the pope as representative of Christ. This is why the ordinary magisterium of the papacy is owed not merely an *actus fidei catholicae*, an act of assent to the authority of the Church, but an *actus fidei divinae*, that assent of faith which is understood as answer to the authority of God himself. Pius XII's view, therefore, is that those subjects on which the pope has staked a position in the exercise of his ordinary magisterium "cannot be any longer considered a question open to discussion among theologians."[9] Accordingly, there has been no dearth of authors seeking to attribute infallibility to the encyclical *Humani Generis*, as will be discussed further on in the context of monogenism.[10] Pius's seriousness in pursuing the ambition stated in *Humani Generis* is attested by the harsh measures against advocates of what he dismissively called *nouvelle théologie*.[11] Henri de Lubac, for example, who would go on to be reintegrated into the hierarchy as a cardinal and who paved the way for Vatican II, lost his professorship in Lyon, along with any teaching responsibilities, only a few months before the issuing of *Humani Generis*.[12]

The uncertainty over the degree to which the papal ordinary magisterium and the encyclical paragraph of *Humani Generis* are binding is also central to understanding many Catholics' despair over the encyclical *Humanae Vitae*, in which Paul VI sternly "condemns" any use of artificial contraceptive methods.[13] There was and is no shortage of theologians ready to declare *Humanae Vitae* infallible.[14]

What is revealing is that those who have denied the infallibility of *Humanae Vitae* have generally done so not on formal grounds—by pointing out that as an exercise of the papal ordinary magisterium, the encyclical is fallible—but rather on material ones, that is, by taking issue with the contents of *Humanae Vitae*. The Würzburg Synod, for example, held that the teachings in *Humanae Vitae*, particularly those on contraception, "are not part of the revealed word and can therefore not be part of infallible Church teaching."[15] The convoluted nature of the argument is telling: rather than failing on the basis of its magisterial presentation, the infallibility of a prohibition on artificial contraception fails because such teaching is not part of revelation. Incidentally, this line of argument would also have been made impossible by the expansion of infallibility in the papacy of John Paul II, as will be discussed further on.

The position, then, is as follows: in the nineteenth century, especially in the context of the Vatican I, the Catholic Church created a highly sophisticated magisterial architecture, the goal of which is to give Church teaching a new form. The feature of this form is that it results from decision-making processes, the outcomes of which are then invested with authority and presented as stemming from revelation. In other words: dogmas are ecclesiastical teaching presented in the form of a ruling, since a dogma represents a *propositio* resulting from a *iudicium*, an authoritative judgment. The fact that this decision form and the authoritative impulse have gained such prominence can be read as a strategic process of modernization.

THE CATHOLIC CHURCH AND MODERNITY

What Does *Modernity* Mean?

The term *modernity* has become so multifaceted over time (and not just recently) that it should be treated with extreme caution. This is not a new insight. As early as 1765, that magnum opus of the French Enlightenment, the *Encyclopédie ou dictionnaire raisonné des sciences, des arts et des métiers* edited by Denis Diderot and Louis de Jaucourt (after the withdrawal of Jean le Rond d'Alembert), contained a listing of the various meanings of the word *modern*:

That which is new, of our time, as opposed to what is *old*....*Modern* coins are those cast less than three hundred years ago....

[Some] call all those authors modern who wrote after Boethius. There has been much discussion on the preeminence of the old over the *modern* writers, and though the latter have many supporters, the first have not lacked for illustrious defenders.

Modern is also used in questions of taste; not in absolute opposition to the old but to that which evinces bad taste: in this way one speaks of modern architecture in contrast with Gothic architecture, even though modern architecture is hardly beautiful, however much it may take on the tastes of antiquity....

Modern astronomy begins with Copernicus... *modern* physics was that of Descartes in the previous century and in this century is that of Newton.[16]

In short, even the encyclopedists of the eighteenth century saw the difficulty that authors today still draw attention to: that "modernity" is a spectrally, temporally, and regionally varied term. Its sense or nonsense depends on the topic, the time, and the place to which it is applied.

Accordingly, there is a wide variety of discourses about modernity that are specific to their various fields. In German literary criticism and theory, where Eugen Wolff first introduced modernity (*die Moderne*) as a term for an era,[17] it is used differently than in empirical sociology, which is concerned with identifying markers of modernization.[18] It is used differently again in systematic theology, where for example there is a debate over how to come to terms with the specifically modern "process of becoming radically aware of the limited nature of human consciousness" and the "historicity of all human thinking."[19] For the sake of organizing the many diverging definitions of the term *modernity*, it seems methodologically useful to distinguish between two approaches. They are nearly impossible to conceive of in their pure form, but they do represent ideal types that can be used for orientation. The first are definitions that place greater weight on the listing of material attributes of modernity; the second are approaches that emphasize formal moments.

A largely material view—at least regarding modernity and religion—is offered by Herbert Schnädelbach.[20] He sees human beings as "cultural being[s]" living in human-made structures of a social, political, or religious nature, which structures are distinct from "the merely natural."[21] According to Schnädelbach, human beings are further capable of becoming aware of their own cultural encodedness through increasing self-reflection. Once a society has reached a defined critical stage of such awareness—to Schnädelbach, the stage in which even recourse to the supposedly natural can be conceived of only in culturally encoded terms—Schnädelbach describes it as "modern," a term he makes normatively charged in reference to religion. "Cultures are fully self-reflecting," he claims,

> once in their self-interpretation they can no longer refer to something that is not cultural and therefore removed from human control—such as demons, gods, and even "nature" [as an entity powerful in itself—Translator]. This is the trademark of modern cultures. In the modern era, culture is completely self-referential in all things; it is its own subject because there is no higher arbiter than the cultural "We." Modern, i.e., fully self-reflecting cultures, are simultaneously profane cultures. Their authorities no longer come from God; rather, all power is given by the people, while everything sacred and pious has retreated into the private sphere. Modern cultures are also of necessity plural cultures, because their "We" lacks the center guiding everything.[22]

Schnädelbach defines modernity in such a way that only those societies can be seen as modern in which religion either no longer plays any public role or does not refer to anything beyond Schnädelbach's "cultural 'We.'" This narrowing of modernity does not necessarily imply an inversely proportional relationship between modernization and religiousness.[23] It is, in fact, possible to conceive of a religious consciousness that understands the historical contingency of how it arose and the fact that it is culturally encoded. Such a consciousness would be self-reflecting in the sense that while—to paraphrase Schnädelbach—it believes in a higher authority beyond the cultural We, it nevertheless views this faith as wholly culturally encoded and recognizes that the higher authority can only be revealed in the guise of the cultural We, in other words, that the natural and the divine can be discussed only as cultural entities.

The problems with Schnädelbach's definition are less theological than historiographical. This is because with his material definition of modernity, Schnädelbach draws far too clear a distinction between premodern (i.e., not self-reflecting, nonprofane, nonplural) societies on the one hand and modern (self-reflecting, profane, plural) societies on the other. This contrast does not stand up to historical scrutiny and is therefore seen as problematic by historians.[24] For not only is one compelled to wonder whether premodern societies were really unable to reflect on the cultural encoding of their recourse to gods, nature, or demons—albeit reflect in a different terminology than that used today—but Shmuel Eisenstadt's concept of multiple modernities also raises the question of whether what Schnädelbach posits as characteristics of modern societies, such as self-reflection, profanity, and plurality, are not themselves contingent in their coexistence. In other words, it is entirely possible to conceive of a society that is highly profane but not plural, or plural but not profane.[25] Is such a society then a modern, premodern, nonmodern, or partially modern society?

These difficulties of a primarily material definition of modernity can be at least partly avoided by treating modernity as a mobile category with strictly defined formal elements. While such a mobile category still contains some normative implications, it at least avoids the strict distinction between epochs.[26] Volker H. Schmidt has developed such an approach, though in his treatment it remains too determined by material concerns and teleological orientations. He seeks to cast modernity "in fairly general terms and place it on a high level of abstraction. Modernity is then not a *state* that can be reached once and for all, however such a state may be defined, but rather a kind of *moving target* that opens the present to a continuously redefined future and urges transformation with reference to this future."[27] Modernity in this sense describes not an epoch, but a "continuum of transformation"[28] that can take on varying degrees of intensity at different times. The past 250-odd years of European history since the Enlightenment are thus modern, not necessarily because they gave rise to phenomena that had been altogether unknown previously. Rather, they are modern because over this period a new philosophical, theological, political, and social dynamic gained momentum. This dynamic did not emerge out of nowhere, but it did exert a hitherto-unknown pressure for change on preexisting conditions and in many cases did indeed manage to change those conditions.

A definition of modernity as a mobile category, then, can no longer be accused of separating the achievements of modernity from its "modern European origins" through a process of "abstractions," turning modernity into "a spatio-temporally neutral model for processes of social development in general," or even severing "the internal connections between modernity and the historical context of Western rationalism," as Habermas had criticized.[29] Quite the contrary: especially if one takes seriously the historical developments of recent centuries in all their complexity and contextuality, one must not make a hard-and-fast, ahistorical distinction between premodernity and modernity, but must perceive the similarities and gray areas between the two. This is most successful when modernity is understood not as an isolated novelty but as a previously unreached degree of intensity: dynamics that may have already existed in premodern societies have reached a never-before-seen momentum. Premodern societies are premodern, however, because these dynamics failed to reach the same pitch to which they have grown over the past 250 years.

Back in his day, the Enlightenment thinker Jean le Rond d'Alembert, of the aforementioned *Encyclopédie*, already distilled this formulation into the metaphor of *fermentation dans les esprits*, fermentation of spirits.

> By its nature, this fermentation acts in all directions, and has engulfed with great violence everything in its path, like a river bursting its dikes....And from the principles of natural science to the foundations of revelation, from metaphysics to matters of taste, from music to morality, from theologians' learned disputes to points of trade, from the rights of princes to those of the people, from natural law to that made for the state...everything has been discussed, analyzed, stirred up.[30]

D'Alembert's metaphor of a violent fermentation that gradually seizes everything in its path is an ambivalent one. It shows how controversial the dynamics of the change are that has grown in power since the eighteenth century. After all, fermentation can improve a substrate, such as when grape juice is turned into wine, or it can destroy it, such as when poorly stored wine becomes vinegar. Modernity, at any rate, has not yet sought to stop its processes of fermentation at a particular point that is meant to be preserved. Instead, it has transformed even the apparently necessary, the definitive, the immutable into moving targets. This has particularly large repercussions for the field of religion, with its claims to special authority over the necessary, definitive, and immutable.

The "Fermentation of Spirits" and Belief in God

If modernity is to be understood as a continuum of transformation with different degrees of intensity and speed, it is nevertheless noticeable how quickly and profoundly the intellectual context in which Christian denominations articulated their truth claims changed from the late eighteenth century onward.[31] Christianity became threatened on the one hand by the rise of historical criticism and on the other by the crisis of natural theology—which had largely attempted to anchor its proofs of God in theoretical rationality.[32]

A decidedly atheistic criticism of religion arose in France in the circle of *encyclopédistes*—Voltaire's deism and the moral charging of religion in Rousseau's work notwithstanding. It was in France that one of the most widely discussed religio-philosophical works of the eighteenth century, *La christianisme dévoilé*, was published in 1766, most likely penned by Paul Thiry d'Holbach. The author wrote, "All religions state that they have come down from the heavens; all prohibit the use of reason to examine their title to sanctity; all make pretensions of truth to the exclusion of others; all threaten with God's wrath those who refuse to submit to their authority; in the end, all have the nature of falsehood."[33] It is a peculiarity of the German Enlightenment that, unlike its French counterpart, it proceeded "in large measure not against theology and Church, but with it and through it."[34] This is true primarily of the Protestant but also of the Catholic Church and is one reason why the German Enlightenment remained on the whole more moderate in its criticism of religion than did the French Enlightenment. Not infrequently, German Enlightenment religious criticism actually sought to provide a new, firm, and altogether better foundation for religion.[35] For based on the discourse at the end of the eighteenth century, there were two aspects that no longer seemed to provide such a foundation: proofs of God and reference to historical processes such as Jesus's miracles or the miraculous spread of the Church.

Kant's objection to proofs of God's existence—proofs that had still been in use in the philosophy of Leibniz and Wolff—was that they demand a kind of use of reason that the human mind cannot fulfill: "All synthetic principles of reason allow only of an immanent employment; and in order to have knowledge of a supreme being we would have to put them to a transcendent use, for which our understanding is in no way fitted."[36] For Kant, therefore, all types of proof that claim to firmly demonstrate the existence of God to the eye of theoretical reason are

17

doomed to fail. According to his categorization, there are three such types: the physico-theological, the cosmological, and the ontological proofs of God's existence. In Kant's view, the existence of God cannot be recognized in theory but only hoped for in practice. Because if we find that what must go together in a moral world—namely, deserving happiness because of adhering to morality and then actually being happy—does not, in fact, go together in our experience; that is, if people who act morally can nevertheless become unhappy by doing so, this raises the question of whether it is enough to rely on "the nature of the things of the world."[37] Kant therefore thinks that the link between happiness and deserving

> can be counted upon only if a *Supreme Reason*, that governs according to moral rules, be likewise posited as underlying nature as its cause. The idea of such an intelligence in which the most perfect moral will, united with supreme blessedness, is the cause of all happiness in the world—so far as happiness stands in exact relation with morality, that is, with worthiness to be happy—[Kant calls]...the *ideal of the supreme good*.[38]

In this conception, God, the union of morality and blessedness as the supreme original good ensures the supreme derivative good, which is that human beings should experience the correspondence between morality and happiness. This makes God's existence a postulate "which...[is] inseparable from the obligation which...reason imposes on us."[39] However, this obligation arises not as an insight of theoretical reason, which would produce knowledge, but by reflection of practical reason on the preconditions moral action requires. Kant does not dispense with God, but he does oust him from the sphere of certain knowledge into the realm of things to be hoped for. As Kant himself confesses, this need not shake the assurance of faith, but does change the epistemic status of the supposition that God exists.[40] God can no longer be an object of potential insight for theoretical reason, but becomes an ordering idea, a *focus imaginarius* that presents reason with the ideal of supreme unity.[41] In practical reason, God becomes a postulate whose existence cannot be recognized but must nevertheless be postulated in order to act morally.[42] Accordingly, theology takes on a new place among scholarly disciplines, moving from metaphysics to the field of ethics. Though this shift had begun already before Immanuel Kant, he was to become its most prominent advocate. Particularly in Protestantism, but also within the Catholic Enlightenment, the shift led to an "ethicization of dogmatics,"[43] which attempted to interpret faith through the lens of moral-philosophical reflection. The crisis engulfed not merely the relationship between faith in God and what could rationally be known about that God, but also the link between Christian faith and the picture that theology sought to draw of that faith's history. In contrast, Augustine, characteristically and definitively for medieval and early modern theology, had rhapsodized about the *ubera historiae*, the "maternal breast of history" as a God-given source of insight.[44]

Augustine concludes that since Christians not only profess God's existence as a metaphysical fact but also singular occurrences resulting from God's love for his creation, culminating in the incarnation of Christ, Christianity cannot refrain from historical reflection. History, understood as a series of examples, provides the concrete instances that allow its students to derive general truths. According to Augustine, history is the very first, most basic step on the path to Christian knowledge of God. It is through prophecies, covenants, fulfilling of same, and miracles, as well as through the spread of the Church, that God has affirmed the truth of the Christian religion; and Augustine believes that this affirmation is accessible through *cognitio historica*, that is, a knowledge of history.[45] Over the course of the eighteenth century, it became increasingly doubtful that one could use history in such a way. There were two reasons for this doubt: The first was increasing skepticism against both the plausibility of supernatural miracles and Christianity's claim to a tradition of prophecy fulfilled. The second was a general questioning of the idea that there could be such a thing as a *cognitio historica* at all. As Lessing put it, "Coincidental historical truths can never become proofs of necessary reasoned truths."[46] It seemed fundamentally problematic to use historical particularities to derive suprahistorical generalities—quite apart from the fact that Christianity's claim to prophecies and miracles as proofs of truth was seen as logically unsound.

Such philological criticisms of prophecy provoked remarkably heated counter-reactions, as evidenced by the Isenbiehl Case. It is all but forgotten today but in the eighteenth century sparked a seismic conflict within the German Church, pitting scholarly interpretation of Scripture against the claims of the papal magisterium, Catholic office holders with Enlightenment sympathies against those critical of the Enlightenment.[47] Johann Lorenz Isenbiehl had merely adopted the thesis—which he himself had not even originated—that the Old Testament prophecy of Isaiah concerning a young woman who would give birth to a son she would name Emmanuel (cf. Isa 7:14) "referred neither to Mary nor to the Messiah."[48] But in doing so, Isenbiehl had disarrayed the internal biblical network of prophecies whose consistency was used in apologetics.

Such use arose because Matthew unequivocally quotes the aforementioned passage in Isaiah in reference to Mary, whom he describes as a virgin, and her son Jesus as the prophesied Messiah (Matt 1:22ff.). To the Church faction inimical to the Enlightenment, headed by Pope Pius VI, it was unacceptable that Matthew might have erred in making this claim to Isaiah's prophecy, as it would have meant a wholesale breakdown of historical apologetics, with its pattern of prefiguring prophecy and fulfilled revelation.[49] Those in Enlightenment-friendly circles, on the other hand, such as Franz Oberthür, praised that Isenbiehl brought "such sagacious criticism" and "such healthy power of discernment" to bear on the Bible that they considered Isenbiehl's reading to be "the only true explanation" of the controversial passage in Isaiah.[50]

Enlightenment thinkers received support for this position from powerful voices within the German episcopate, such as

Johann Nikolaus von Hontheim, alias *Febronius*, and Karl Theodor von Dalberg, who was later to become bishop of the united sees of Constance, Worms, Mainz, and Ratisbon/Regensburg. Such figures had no interest in an expansion of the power of the papal magisterium and therefore protected theologians critical of Rome. The Isenbiehl case is an incisive example of how critical Bible exegesis—which in the seventeenth century had been used by Catholic-adjacent theologians to attack the principle of *sola scriptura*—came to be adopted, fine tuned, and radicalized by Protestant Enlightenment theology until it reentered the Catholic Church in the late eighteenth century, stoking conflict.[51] The Church of the time could find no other way of dealing with such conflict than to bolster its authority.

The methodology of biblical criticism, which researches the historical context and original meaning of statements as well as the formal or factual breaks in the historical transmission of texts and ideas, gained scope as it was adopted by Protestant theology: it was applied no longer merely to the Bible, but to the doctrines of faith as well. In the light of such a methodology, the orthodox conception of teaching—whether of a Catholic, Lutheran, or Reformed bent—came to be viewed as the contingent result of historical processes, as a point in the convoluted line of *historia dogmatum* shaped by injustices and misunderstandings, as Johann Jerusalem first put it in 1747.[52] Deprived of a sense of its teleological necessity and apodictic immutability, traditional doctrine was subjected to discussion of its content, such that doctrinal truth was no longer simply taken for granted but interrogated as to its justification. And where such justification could no longer be found, moves were made to challenge and change doctrine. And so the standard Enlightenment repertoire soon included criticism of the doctrines of original sin, penal substitution, dyophysitism, and even the Trinity.[53]

This awareness of contingency—that is, the insight that even doctrinal religious traditions were not bound to be as they are, and that even the existence of God remains worth questioning—

fundamentally changed the intellectual and social framework in which the Christian religion moved after the Enlightenment.

Changing Demands on Religion

One should be wary of phrases that preface the word *society* with a descriptor—as in "consumer society," "throwaway society," or "selfish society." They tend to reduce the complexity of social processes to a single aspect—in the examples, consumerism, throwing away, or selfishness, respectively. But on occasion, such coinages can be helpful. In one instance, Uwe Schimank titled his volume on the "complexity and rationality of the modern era" with the German word *Entscheidungsgesellschaft*, meaning "decision society." According to Schimank, actors in modern society, be they organizations or individuals, are faced with the challenge of having to "conceive and complete ever more actions, and especially the important ones, as decisions."[54] Schimank does not consider every type of action to take the form of a decision, instead distinguishing between different kinds of action. He is not interested in the internal mental processes preceding an action—in such a case, the act of deciding would by definition be linked to an action, since decision-making would be understood as the result of arriving at a will that is then equipped with motivating force so that it finds expression in action. Instead, Schimank considers the societal conditions that constitute decision-making. In so doing, he distinguishes true decisional action from routine, traditional, or emotional actions. The last category is unimportant here, but from a theological standpoint, routine and tradition are worth investigating. "Social routines are prescriptions for correct behavior that have been made through decisions."[55] Such routine action shapes the use of liturgy, for example. Traditional action, meanwhile, occurs in situations closely defined by the relevant society. It is guided by "clear normative and cognitive expectations, as have been [established] in lived social relationships."[56] The baptism of a newborn is thus not a routine action for the parents because—even in families with a large number of children—it simply occurs too rarely. Throughout most of the history of European Christendom, however, it was an expression of traditional action: while it was theoretically possible that the child of Catholic or Protestant parents might not be baptized, in practice such an occurrence was far outside the realm of the socially conceivable or acceptable.

Applying the concept of traditional action to theology, one may say the following: after the Protestant Reformation, different ideas of Church teaching came to be established based on the different religious denominations. These ideas became increasingly fixed as the denominations solidified in the early modern period. Thereafter, theologians generally engaged in traditional action whenever they adopted these ideas of their own denomination. For example, it was not an everyday occurrence for a seventeenth-century Protestant scholar to deny the material inerrancy of Scripture nor for a Catholic theologian of the same time to reject the sacrament of penance and reconciliation in the shape of personal, private confession. In the rare cases in which such deviation occurred, it was sanctioned. Theologians thus hardly needed to decide whether or not Scripture was inerrant or the sacrament of penance tied to private confession. Instead, they could concentrate on the question of why things were as their particular denomination taught them or how their own denomination's teachings might be even more plausibly justified.

> Decisional action becomes increasingly pointless or unnecessary for an actor as the actionable situation becomes more precisely defined. The decisional action becomes unnecessary to the extent that the situation suggests to the actor a specific path of traditional, routine, or emotional action which would lead to acceptable results in the eyes of the actor....If one looks at poorly defined situations, on the other hand, it becomes clear that these imply simultaneously the need and the opportunity to better cope with the problem through decision-making. At first, such situations produce a more or less drastic disorientation in the actor. They

are experienced as surprising, unforeseen, new, dra-
matic, vague, indistinct, open to interpretation, *et
cetera*—all of which are different ways of expressing
that the actor lacks ready patterns of action.[57]

Such "ready patterns of action" are provided in well-defined
situations by traditional action. In the light of D'Alembert's
"great fermentation" cited above, modernity could be described
as a dynamic that transformed the social form and the magisterial tradition of the various Churches from relatively well-defined
into relatively poorly defined situations. But this thesis is historically valid only if the term *modernity*, as mentioned above, is
understood not as the fixed definition of an epoch but as a flex-
ible interpretive category. In such a way, one can avoid a strict
opposition between premodern, supposedly well-defined and
nondecisional situations and modern, poorly defined situations
calling for decisions.[58] Such an opposition is untenable because
even in periods generally agreed upon to be premodern, there
were open-ended actionable situations in religious matters (such
as the sixteenth-century Reformation and its consequences)
that required profound decision-making by both individuals
and institutions.[59] For example, the Peace of Augsburg granted
the rulers the right to freely decide, within the context of the *ius
reformationis* ("law of reformation") whether they belonged to
the Catholic Church or allied themselves with the Augsburg Confession. Subjects of the rulers, however, were granted the derived
right of *ius emigrandi*, meaning that while they had the right to
reach a different religious decision than their ruler, in such a case
the subjects must further the ideal of a denominationally homo-
geneous state by emigrating to a territory in keeping with their
denomination.[60] For those who stayed, meanwhile, this only
raised the pressure on the decision whether or not to espouse
the denomination of their territory. What began in the first half
of the sixteenth century as a locally ill-defined religious situation
became, over the following decades of internal politics strength-
ening each denomination, once again a well-defined situation

making it possible to again practice religion as traditional action rather than as the result of purposeful decisional action.

What is new about the decisional pressure in religious matters that fermented in the eighteenth century and has only gained strength into the present is its historically unparalleled potency in transforming well-defined into poorly defined situations and the broad scope in which this potency took effect. As a result, particularly the status of the individual as regards religious questions has undergone a fundamental shift. Immanuel Kant expresses this succinctly in "Answer to the Question: What Is Enlightenment?" his famous essay in the December 1784 issue of the *Berlinische Monatsschrift*. In the essay, Kant wonders whether binding rulings can be used to once and for all settle discussions within religious groups.

> [Could a group of clerics] have the right to obligate, under oath, one another to a particular immutable symbol in order to thus hold and even to perpetuate an unending supreme custodianship over each of its members and indirectly through these over the people? I say that this is utterly impossible. Such a contract, which would be made to forever preclude all further enlightenment of the human race is absolutely null and void; for all that it may be affirmed by the ruling power, by parliaments, or by the most solemn peaceful accords. [Or by the Pope, one might be moved to add from a Catholic perspective.—M. S.] One age cannot conspire and swear itself to place the next into a state in which it becomes impossible to...expand its insights, cleanse them of errors, and overall advance further in enlightenment. This would be a crime against the nature of man.[61]

Such a statement has far-reaching consequences for the Catholic Church, which knows itself to be bound to revelation and a particular history of interpretation of said revelation—often referred to as tradition—and which therefore records, for example, a history of its creeds. The Church of today sees the legitimacy of beliefs held within it as bounded by rulings of the past, and where it makes magisterial rulings today, the Church claims to oblige future generations to be bound by present-day teaching. Magisterial rulings by the Church, then, attempt to transform the uncertainty of the future into a certainty that can be captured in the present. This effort is visible in terms such as *definitive, irrevocable,* and *infallible.* Through such a strategy, future conflicts are to be resolved already in the present or—even better from the point of view of those issuing the ruling—prevented from arising in the first place.[62]

Kant rejected the binding nature of transmitted doctrine unless this bindingness could be proved correct through the use of one's own reason. This means that what has been transmitted loses its authoritative character; tradition no longer has any special epistemic position.[63] Tradition persists only where the individual is capable of recognizing it as meaningful and is rejected where the individual can no longer rationally approve it. This antiauthoritarian insistence on the individual as the competent judge in religious questions suggests that modernity, in the dynamic described above, is not merely a directionless continuum of change, but rather contains normative impulses that centrally include self-determination, particularly in religious questions.[64] In two senses, then, the Christian faith became increasingly optional. In the first place, one could belong to a church or not belong to one, as initially informal secular spaces were created in which—as in the early United States of America—despite strong religious activity of most of the population, there existed juridical guarantees of religious freedom. In Europe, these were achieved on a large scale only in the twentieth century.[65] This made and makes religious membership a matter of choice not just in theory but also in practice. (Admittedly, Christianity does cultivate a rhetoric of decision-based repentance, but has also created the institution of child baptism, through which people, by the time they reach the age of discernment and thus decision-making, already find themselves members of a religious denomination without having made the choice.)

But the question of choice is limited not only to the question of whether or not one belongs to a religious denomination. The second way in which religion became optional was that one could selectively take up—or reject—individual teachings of a particular religion. In a society based on separation of church and state and guaranteeing freedom of religion, the Church can not compel its members to believe in the doctrines of the trinity, sacraments, or original sin, however important these themes may be from a theological perspective. The religious sociologist Peter L. Berger has coined the phrase *heretical imperative* to describe this situation, punning on the word *heresy* and its double meaning. The Ancient Greek root *hairesis* means nothing other than "selection." But used in the normative Christian sense, a heretic is a false teacher, someone who selectively adopts Church teaching and distorts them by doing so.

> For the term of heresy to acquire any meaning at all, it required the authority of a religious tradition as its necessary precondition. Only with respect to such an authority could one even take up a heretical position, since the heretic denied this authority and refused to accept the totality of its tradition....One must assume that the possibility of heresy has always and forever existed in human communities, just as one must assume that there have always been rebels and innovators; and certainly those representing the authority of a particular tradition must always have had to find ways to deal with this possibility. With the advent of modernity, however, there has been a radical change in the social context of this phenomenon. In pre-modern societies, people live in a world of religious security which is occasionally damaged by heretical discrepancies. The modern situation, on the other hand, offers a world of insecurity which is occasionally ameliorated by more or less brittle constructs of religious affirmation. In fact, the change can be described even more starkly: For pre-modern people, heresy was a possibility, though usually a remote one. For modern people,

heresy is typically a necessity. Or yet again: modernity creates a new situation in which selection and choice become imperatives.[66]

In general, Berger's analyses are accurate; while they require some additional fine-tuning from a theological point of view, this added precision in fact winds up radicalizing Berger's fundamental thoughts even further. Berger presupposes a largely uniform tradition that is itself invested with authority, or whose integrity is preserved by some institutional authority such as the magisterium of the Catholic Church. Accordingly, these authorities lose their acceptance—an acceptance based on authority, that is, on obedience—through the dynamic of modernity, leading to a selective uptake of tradition. But such an appraisal fails to recognize that tradition in the end is merely a collective noun loaded up with normative significance: tradition is constituted as the result of a process of choice and selection—one might say, of heresy considered orthodox.[67]

The magisterium of the Catholic Church, as well, is not simply the preserver of a given tradition but has actually constituted this tradition itself through decisions that chose one option over another. As a concrete example, those who identify only the Twelve whom Jesus gathered around himself as apostles are making a choice that excludes other conceptions of apostlehood also found in the New Testament, such as those employed by Paul (1 Cor 15:5–8) or given in Hebrews (3:1). And those who further argue that women cannot hold Church offices in apostolic succession because the circle of the Twelve contained no women have loaded this selective reading of the New Testament with far-reaching consequences despite the fact that the relationship between office and sex is discussed nowhere in the New Testament. Succession and poverty, on the other hand, are explicitly considered: "So therefore, none of you can become my disciple if you do not give up all your possessions" (Luke 14:33).

If this applies to all who follow Jesus, should it not apply also to those who live their discipleship by taking Church office?

It could be argued that the link between Church office and poverty is biblically self-evident, but it has played a subordinate role throughout most epochs of Christian history. The link between Church office and sex, on the other hand, is not a subject of New Testament theology and has nevertheless been expanded into a central pillar of the theology of Catholic Church office, especially in recent decades. The magisterium, then, is not a preserver of a tradition it has received, but rather shapes this tradition by determining through its decisions what counts as tradition and what does not. It does so either by claiming the authority to make such choices or by using its authority to deny that it is making a choice at all—that is, by disguising its own decision-making as acting in the name of tradition.

One of modernity's hallmarks, however, is to recognize with its critical consciousness of history the contingent nature of these processes of tradition building. Modernity is no longer willing to accept these results on faith, however much authority they may come clothed in. An action-based way of dealing with contingency—such as magisterial teaching—aims to make the vastness of the possible manageable by using decision-making to allow only a small fraction of the possible to actually be realized. In this sense, the magisterium of the Catholic Church is simply dealing with doctrinal contingency. But not everything that is possible and fails to be realized necessarily becomes impossible. Some options that are possible can continue to accompany the real with varying degrees of intensity, offering themselves up as alternatives—even if only tragically missed, unchosen alternatives.[68] Niklas Luhmann has described this using the originally phenomenological term of *appresentation*: "But since every exclusion must choose a form, must make a distinction, all meaningful action regenerates simultaneously the medium of the other option and lastly the unmarked state of the world which no longer excludes anything. There is always some provisional remainder of something unsaid, so that whatever is determined also remains deconstructible."[69] More succinctly: "Whatever has been excluded is always appresented; whatever is unusable or not operatively connectable is always also implicitly communicated. One can never be certain whether the communication will not somehow/sometime cross boundaries."[70] Modernity allows the individual to become sensitive to the religiously appresented. That is, the forms of religious life and faith that institutions proclaim authoritatively are viewed by modernity as merely one, but not the only possible, form. Accordingly, the individual as competent judge in religious matters is capable of breaking the authority of the Church simply by no longer recognizing it.

The Church, which has an interest in the integrity of what it pronounces as tradition, can react to such a breach in two ways: it can either give an explication of its doctrine by offering reasons and seeking the approval of the individual (in the hope that faith in God can be presented in terms of reason); or it can raise its claim to authority (in the hope that modernity's skepticism toward authority can be reined in by greater authority). To a certain extent, it has made use of both of these ways.[71] But it has gone significantly further in the second—that is, in raising its claim to authority.

THE MAGISTERIUM:
A MODERN CONSTRUCT

The foregoing may have served at least to suggest why the magisterial structure of the Catholic Church as described above, encompassing an ordinary and extraordinary magisterium that can be exercised collectively or through primacy, arose. The magisterium, so far from being a way of teaching handed down since time immemorial, is actually a sign of modernization. More precisely, it is a teaching construct that was strategically sensitive to modernity, with the aim of presenting Church teachings as dogma, that is, in the form of rulings and sanctioned by official authority.

The idea that in addition to the solemn magisterium of the Councils there might also be an ordinary magisterium, exercised constantly by the pope and binding for all, is an "invention" of Joseph Kleutgen in the mid-nineteenth century.[72] Its goal was to give the pope the power and authority necessary to develop a strategic response appropriate to modernity—with all its new decision-making pressures—without having to normatively concede to modernity on each individual's competency to make religious decisions independently. Kleutgen developed his idea of an ordinary magisterium in discussion with Johann Baptist Hirscher, a theologian who taught first in Tübingen and later in Freiburg. Hirscher, for his part, complained of "an obsessive compulsion [to call] heretical" even those who simply "deviate from the conventional notions of the theologians" or employ "a different terminology" without actually running counter to the "concept of teaching (as it is defined by the Church)."[73]

According to Hirscher, as long as a theologian did not contradict what the solemn, conciliar magisterium of the Church had decreed (the papal solemn magisterium was, after all, not defined until Vatican I), that theologian was not a heretic. This is not to say that Hirscher represented a laissez-faire theological approach—quite the contrary. Simply stating that a theological thesis is not heretical does not make it correct. Outside of orthodoxy or heterodoxy, however, Hirscher wanted to leave the truth or falsity of a theological position up to theological debate rather than to authoritative intervention on the part of the magisterium. Kleutgen reacted to this criticism from 1853 onward in his theology of prehistory, simultaneously expounding a new conception of the Church magisterium. Kleutgen argued that it was a mistake to think of theology as free beyond what had already been ruled by the solemn magisterium. Rather, the Church exercised

> a double magisterium. One is the ordinary and eternal....The other is extraordinary, exercised only at special time, to wit, when false teachers unsettle the Church, and is not merely the office of teaching but simultaneously of judging. In this latter [magisterium], the Church defends against the inimical attacks on the hallows which she preserves; in the other she opens

up to her children the rich treasures which are laid up within her.[74]

Kleutgen even denies that the solemn, extraordinary magisterium is a magisterium in the strict sense. What, for example, the Councils do, he opines, was rather a kind of judging, whereas the true magisterium was the ordinary magisterium—in other words, the one invented by Kleutgen himself—through which the Church made revelation accessible to the faithful.

This conception results in a significant change in the relationship between the episcopal magisterium, which Kleutgen assigns exclusively to the pope, and the doctoral magisterium—the teaching duties of the theologians. Where it had previously been the task of theologians to use contemporary thought to unearth what Kleutgen referred to as the rich treasure with which the Church was entrusted and then to intellectually buff up the treasure until it shone, where previously the bishops had been limited to interceding with solemn Councils when faith was threatened with utter distortion, Kleutgen now suggested transferring the proactive aspect of teaching onto the pope.[75] This turned the pope into a kind of supertheologian whose rulings would henceforth form the *regula proxima fidei* that theologians would then have to interpret. Meanwhile, Scripture and tradition became *regulae remotae fidei* that one would no longer need to consult as a theologian if the pope had already spoken.[76]

Pope Pius IX took up this theological conception for the first time in 1863 in his epistle *Tuas libenter*, which was directed at the *Münchener Gelehrtenversammlung*, a Munich conference of theologians critical of the doctrine of infallibility. Under the influence of Ignaz von Döllinger, the Munich conference attempted to confront the neoscholastic monopolization of theology in the hands of the Vatican, demanding academic freedom for theologians, especially regarding their methodologies. As the pope saw it, through their criticism "the authority of the Church itself [was] called into question."[77] Pius insisted that the requirement of *fide divina*—divine faith—"should not be limited to the things expressly determined by decrees of the ecumenical Councils or the Roman Bishops and this Apostolic Seat" but also to the pronouncements of the ordinary magisterium.[78] In other words, he claimed, through the ordinary magisterium—an idea that had at that time existed for all of ten years—God himself was speaking. Consequently, the statements of the ordinary magisterium should be accorded the same obedience as required in answer to God's revelation. But Pius IX went even further, expressly prescribing the curia as taking part in papal authority by extending the authority of the magisterium to the "papal congregations" as well.[79]

Several years later, the First Vatican Council affirmed the implementation of the ordinary magisterium—and thus an unprecedented expansion of papal authority—and invested it with the requisite juridical power. The Council agreed with Pius IX on his view, which "[reduced] the modern world to a denial of the authority of the hierarchical Church" and attempted to increase precisely this authority as a countermove.[80] In the process, the pope's teaching power was explicitly reflected in the category of decision-making. According to Klaus Schatz, the ultimately successful infallibilist faction, which advocated the papacy's ability to exercise the solemn magisterium through papal primacy, foregrounded "the dimension of *decision*" in its considerations; whereas the anti-infallibilist minority was guided by "the term '*testimony*'" and understood the function of the magisterium as limited to "testifying to the faith handed down."[81] More on this distinction below. Here it will suffice to point out that under the category of testimony, the duties of the magisterium are epistemic: it must recognize and testify to what the Church believes. The category of decision, in contrast, implies that teaching could take several different potential forms, with the pope being the final arbiter over which form is implemented. This, in turn, implies that the forms not chosen by the pope—and thus not realized—are thenceforth only to be thought of as heresies.

Hermann Josef Pottmeyer has thoroughly examined the ways in which the papal magisterium was designed first and foremost from the point of view of sovereignty in the First Vatican Council. In the process, the theological question of testifying to faith handed down was largely subordinated. Notwithstanding a number of cautionary voices that will be discussed below, to the ultimately successful majority within the Council, infallibility appeared primarily as a "question of constitutional policy."[82] In the face of the modern conception of sovereignty that applied in the political arena of nineteenth-century nation-states and included the power to make laws and rule on them, the project was to present the pope as Church sovereign, in whom all authority and *potestas* came together in a manner that would be juridically binding for all members. An early representative of this movement was Joseph de Maistre, whose 1819 treatise *Du pape* propagated— starting from the notion of sovereignty in the political realm—the idea of "papal infallibility, which was advocated almost nowhere else anymore."[83] He was thus to decisively shape theology leading up to Vatican I, where, in the words of Pottmeyer, the pope was elevated from "testifier to monarch" in a manner that previous papal tradition had by no means prefigured:

> What therefore played out in the rise of the Pope to become monarch of the Church was not the logical or organic development of the Petrine idea or consistent realization of the Petrine mission. Rather, this rise was part of the development in the Church's consciousness of itself as not just preserver of and testifier to a legacy but also active shaper of this legacy—in modern terms, as an active subject of its own story. That was the development behind the "development" of the office of Peter to the point of a monarchic primate. It was a one-sided development because the Church's new self-consciousness encoded itself primarily in the pope.[84]

From then on, the papacy's solemn power to issue laws and rulings also extended to the magisterium, which the pope was now empowered to exercise both ordinarily and extraordinarily on his own, without being bound to the consensus of the bishops, much less the entire Church. Papal infallibility in dogmatic questions was so far subjugated to papal primacy in juridical questions that the magisterial pope appeared merely as a particular aspect of the legislating pope—a figure on the same level as worldly sovereigns and trying to counter his loss of authority in the context of modernity by claiming the *plenitudo potestatis*, the full range of powers, conceivable within the Church. The result of this process was that the teaching of faith came to be increasingly juridical in ways that persist to this day. The case of Matthias Joseph Scheeben is just one example of such "juridicalization." In order to incorporate the results of Vatican I as fully as possible, Scheeben had reworked his *Theologische Erkenntnislehre* (Theological epistemology) numerous times before its printing in 1873. This made it one of the first systematic and large-scale presentations of the Council rulings in German-speaking areas. In the text, Scheeben attempted to do what the First Vatican Council had been unable to do because of its suspension and eventual indefinite adjournment: integrate the new rulings on papal infallibility with Catholic dogmatics as a whole. In so doing, Scheeben conceived of the pope's infallibility mainly in juridical categories. Any papal teaching represented, in his words, "an act of a judge's jurisdiction" presenting "the law of faith," for which reason the pope's teachings were to be accorded both "an outer legal force" and an "inner legal force."[85]

Accordingly, the 1917 *Codex Iuris Canonici* (*Code of Canon Law*)—another project seeking to present the pope as a sovereign lawgiver in analogy with the heads of nation-states but counter to canon law precedent—developed magisterial laws that spelled out the juridically binding nature of papal pronouncements of faith. In tandem, it also defined criticism of papal readings as a criminal offense and determined corresponding sanctions.[86]

While the current *Code of Canon Law* is structured differently, it has retained the offenses against the faith. Likewise retained—because desirable to the magisterium—is the mentality of a juridicalization of the teachings of faith, even to the extent of removing certain subjects on which the magisterium has spoken from the purview of dogmatic theology altogether and integrating them into canon law as if that were the actually pertinent discipline. For example, when there is discussion of the ordination of women, and a dogmatic theologian opines that the possibility of ordaining women remains open for debate, a canonist will respond by explaining that there is definitively nothing more to be said, since the topic—a matter of faith—has been finally decided with legally binding force.[87] This raises the question: Why do theology at all when there is a pope who decides what is right and canonists who will codify this decision into law and define offenses accordingly?

The Second Vatican Council does not undo the magisterial architecture set up by Vatican I, but it does attempt to translate it into a different context, since Vatican II is no longer primarily interested in establishing the pope as sovereign of the Church. Instead, it attempts to integrate the pope and his infallibility—which *Lumen Gentium* does not dispute, and, in fact, explicitly reasserts in paragraph 18—into the Church at large.[88] This is done in the first place by centering the episcopal college.[89] The community of bishops scattered all across the world, in this context, is cast as the first body of infallible teaching (in the sense of the collegially exercised ordinary magisterium). The pope—styled expressly as Bishop of Rome and thus both part and head of this college—is cast as the second instantiation of infallible teaching (in the sense of the extraordinary magisterium exercised through papal primacy), before the community of bishops (in the sense of the collegially exercised solemn magisterium) is then once again foregrounded, at least so long as it is convened in an ecumenical council. This inclusion, which is characteristic of *Lumen Gentium* 25, is by no means an accident: the pope as a bishop is set at the center of the college whose head he is.

Vatican II's other strategy for embedding the doctrine of infallibility in the Church at large consists of placing the faithful ahead of episcopal teaching as a whole, since the faithful (through baptism and confirmation) take part in joint priesthood and thus in the *tria munera Christi*, Christ's priestly, prophetic, and kingly office.[90] The communion of all baptized Christians is thus the actual foundation of all teaching, since the Church entire, not merely its isolated hierarchy, is considered *indefectabilis*:

> The holy people of God shares also in Christ's prophetic office [Christ's teaching office, i.e., his magisterium—-M.S.]; it spreads abroad a living witness to Him, especially by means of a life of faith and charity and by offering to God a sacrifice of praise, the tribute of lips which give praise to His name. The entire body of the faithful, anointed as they are by the Holy One, cannot err in matters of belief.[91]

This phrasing by the Council is remarkable. The juridicalization of the teaching of faith as propagated after Vatican I—with the *munus docendi*, the teaching office or magisterium, understood as a facet of the pope's sovereign *munus regendi*, or reigning office—is tacitly corrected: rather than the kingly office, *Lumen Gentium* now discusses the prophetic office.

Moreover, the constitution states that inerrant faith—which in a binary logic would be considered equivalent to infallibility—can be presented not only in propositional rulings, but also *per vitam fidei et caritatis*, through a life of faith and charity.[92] The truth of faith is thus no longer delineated as something that can be stated and thus must be accepted or denied on a propositional level, but as something that can be lived. Truth can be not only spoken, but also done—in the spirit of the Gospel of John: "But those who do what is true come to the light, so that it may be clearly seen that their deeds have been done in God" (John 3:21). It is precisely this kind of teaching by living that the constitution interprets as participation in the prophetic office of Christ.

Neither of the Second Vatican Council's two strategies for embedding papal teaching in the larger Church—neither the localization of the pope within the episcopal college nor the centering of the faithful—was taken up effectively in the juridical implementation of the Council. This is all the more lamentable since canon law is the discipline that defines the place of the rest of theology within the Church. The *Code of Canon Law*, in its reworking after Vatican II, leaves the pope in a splendid isolation regarding religious teaching. Where the Council named first the episcopal college and then the pope, in his function as head of that college, as the subjects of infallibility, the new *Codex Iuris Canonici* names first the pope—"in a conscious omission of his position within the college of bishops"—and then the bishops, though not without "expressing their connection with the Petrine successor and the Roman Bishop a full two times."[93]

Postconciliar magisterial developments, however, have not been content to ignore the options opened up by Vatican II. Instead, the magisterium has countercorrected the Council in crucial questions. As defined by the First Vatican Council, the only matters that could possibly be subjects to infallible teaching were those "which [were] contained in the written or handed-down word of God" and could therefore be considered to have been revealed.[94] After the Council was suspended, the question of whether those matters not themselves explicitly revealed but considered linked with the revelation could also be subjects of infallible teaching was not resolved. It remained open.[95] Nor did the Second Vatican Council take up the idea that nonrevealed matters might be subjects of infallible teaching. The draft document *De Ecclesia*, presented to the fathers on November 23, 1962, contained a far-reaching interpretation of papal infallibility that would have gone significantly beyond Vatican I. *De Ecclesia* claims that it pertains to the magisterium to interpret not merely revelation but all of nature as the whole of nonrevelation and domain of reason in a comprehensive sense (*non modo revelatam sed et naturalem legem interpretandi*), so that there is finally no realm of human action or experience that is ultimately removed from the reach of magisterially infallible overview: *Nulla est ergo provincia humanarum actionum, quae sub adspectu ethico et religioso auctoritati magisterii a Christo instituti subtrahi possit.*[96] This sentence, along with the entire prepared draft, was rejected by the Council fathers and is not found in the constitution, which instead clearly and unequivocally limits the applicability of infallible teaching to revelation.

Lumen Gentium states that the "infallibility with which the Divine Redeemer willed His Church to be endowed in defining doctrine of faith and morals, extends as far as the deposit of Revelation extends."[97] According to conciliar teaching, the Church can therefore rule infallibly on anything which is revealed—and conversely, on only those things that are revealed.

This limitation was initially to be included in the 1983 revision of the *Code of Canon Law*. In the final editing stage, however, it was once again struck out in an attempt to meet the "crisis of acceptance of Church authority" with another expansion of one's own claim to authority.[98] In the following years, the purview of infallible teaching was expanded even further in a manner covered by neither the First nor the Second Vatican Council.[99] The Profession of Faith from 1989, for example, implies that even what the ordinary magisterium rules on matters not themselves revealed may be proclaimed by a definitive act and must therefore be adhered to and maintained.[100] Through the apostolic letter *Ad Tuendam Fidem* issued *motu proprio* in 1998, Pope John Paul II even adopted this dogmatic innovation into canon law by changing the *Code* after the fact. To §750, he added a second paragraph decreeing that even that which was not revealed but which from a magisterial point of view was "required for the holy keeping and faithful exposition of the deposit of faith" must be definitively held and that "anyone who rejects propositions which are to be held definitively sets himself against the teaching of the Catholic Church."[101] John Paul II also altered canon 1371, which deals with "delicts against ecclesiastical authorities" by adding provisions that those who deny nonrevealed teaching proclaimed with definitive intent shall be "punished with a just penalty."[102] Far from protecting revelation, the Church is here protecting revelation perhaps least of all, and instead upholding the authority of the Church leadership, as the positioning within the *Code* makes clear. This particular canon is not located among the delicts against religion and the unity of the Church, but merely in Title II, concerned with "delicts against ecclesiastical authorities." Indeed, it is preceded by the penalties for using physical force against the pope, a bishop, or another cleric. Evidently, critical thinking in the face of authority is similarly culpable.

The 1992 *Catechism of the Catholic Church*, the stated aim of which is "presenting an organic synthesis of the essential and fundamental contents of Catholic doctrine...in the light of...the whole of the Church's Tradition" also recapitulates developments in the conception of teaching during the pontificate of John Paul II in its discussion of dogma.[103] If the idea of dogma, ever since it arose, had been bound firmly to revelation so that the First and Second Vatican Councils (in *Dei Filius* and *Lumen Gentium* respectively, as shown above) still held that only revealed matters could be authoritatively proclaimed as dogma, the *Catechism of the Catholic Church* blithely leaves these Councils behind, creating a new form of dogma: "The Church's Magisterium exercises the authority it holds from Christ to the fullest extent when it defines dogmas, that is, when it proposes truths contained in divine Revelation or also when it proposes in a definitive way truths having a necessary connection with them."[104]

The end of this sentence could hardly be more consequential: it dissolves the exclusive binding of dogma to revelation. Dogmas can now also include the teachings pertaining to matters that even the magisterium freely admits as not themselves revealed but only connected with revealed matters. This connection, John Paul II states in *Ad Tuendam Fidem*, may arise "either for historical reasons or by a logical relationship."[105] What is historically linked with doctrine is no longer up for theological debate but is subject to the authoritative decision of the pope, who can then even proclaim his personal assessment of the case as dogma. Thus, one of the two original constitutive aspects of dogma—its revealed nature—was not merely weakened but eliminated wholesale in favor of its other original constitutive aspect, the proclamation by authority.

Faith in a proper theological sense refers to the answer to divine revelation, not to the authority of the Church. There are now therefore, as Joseph Ratzinger himself has explained, dogmas that paradoxically cannot in the strictest sense be believed as faith. They belong not to the *fides credenda* but—at best—to the *fides tenenda*. They are categorized in "the second level of the Profession, the truths to be held definitively, but not actually to be embraced with the full belief of faith."[106]

THE MAGISTERIAL ARCHITECTURE OF THE CHURCH II

This chapter began with an outline of the current architecture of the magisterium of the Catholic Church, concluding that this architecture should be understood as phenomenon of modernization. Then followed a discussion what modernity might mean in the present context: a continuum of transformation exhibiting a tendency to criticize the authority of religious institutions by revealing the historical contingency of all that exists. The individual is thus given the possibility of taking a decisive stance on religious questions, leading to a specific set of demands on religious institutions in the modern era. They had to learn to respond adequately to criticism of their claims to authority and to do justice to the heightened general awareness of historical contingency and the increased room for choice it gave their members. Having called attention to these aspects of what one might call the "modern condition" of religion, the chapter subsequently sought to show how much the Church's articulation of its magisterial architecture owes to such modernity. The magisterium took up the challenges modernity posed by trying to cast Church teaching into the form of dogmatic teaching—that is, by increasingly presenting Church teaching in the form of decisions invested with ever greater amounts of authority. Schnädelbach's dictum thus holds true for the Church as well:

> Modernity is not a project, but it does force us to keep taking up projects, because in modernity, the crucial things can no longer be taken for granted and even the anti-modern "leaving it be"...[and similar defensive strategies—M.S.] are our projects. Specifically, anti-projects. We cannot

get away from modernity, since even anti-modernity would be a modern project.[107]

The first step toward reform of the Church under the aegis of theology is therefore to recognize the specific modernness of the Church. Demanding any particular change based on the frequently uttered watchword of "modernization" is vague and even misleading. Reforms do not need to modernize the Church because it is already modern. The question is whether the already completed modernization of the Catholic Church was successful or whether there might be reasons to position the Christian faith differently in the present than it is currently positioned. This historicization is the only way to overcome the false dichotomy of a normatively overloaded status quo on the one hand and supposedly heretical reformational departures from it on the other. Because on closer inspection, it turns out that the magisterial status quo that the Catholic Church likes to imbue with an aura of the inevitably given is actually fairly new. The development of the concept of dogma under John Paul II is merely one example of how this status quo dates to only the most recent period of history.

The Protestant theologian Gerhard Ebeling showed how well he understood the Catholic Church when he wrote that Catholicism was shaped by "a double tendency [toward] a radical conservatism and a no less radical evolutionism" simultaneously.[108] In order to preserve the facade of a conservatism that pretends to keep everything as it has always been, the Catholic Church has given itself over to a particular kind of evolutionism. Part of the strategy of such evolution is to conceal itself—or to use the terminology developed above, to disguise acts of decision-making as acts of tradition. A theology that is skeptical of such historical politics must aim to uncover this disguise. That way, the question of the appropriate shape of the Church today can be discussed without recourse to dummy constructs.

3

CHURCH TEACHING AND MAGISTERIAL LEARNING

EPISTEMIC AND JURIDICAL AUTHORITY I

The term *authority* has at least three facets, each of which is legitimate in its context and indispensable in both society and the Church. Aristotle, at the beginning of his *Topics*, distinguishes among various modes of drawing conclusions. In the first place, there are conclusions drawn from apodictic reasoning. These arise from premises whose truth is not in doubt and are therefore demonstrably certain. Besides these, there are also conclusions drawn from dialectical reasoning, which are based on premises that are only probably true.[1] These include, for example, statements by those recognized to be wise. The authority of the wise, in this case, has an epistemic function. In a situation of cognitive uncertainty, those seeking insight turn to some source which, for good reasons, they trust to be able to testify to the truth.

"The authority linked to testimony is an extrinsic source of justification, and in the philosophical tradition is often contrasted with reason as an 'intrinsic' source of knowledge. In the social context of evaluating testimony, the expression 'epistemic authority' should be understood as a type of authority through which a person is recognized as knowledgeable."[2] It is thus not the producer of truth but its witness who holds authority, and this witness is not required where truth is plain to see even without authority. Conversely, this means that authority can never make any inroads against a truth already recognized by those who are questioning the authority. For the moment an authority makes a statement against the better knowledge of those consulting it as an authority, it loses its status as epistemic authority: as a source making obviously false claims, it can no longer for good reasons be considered knowledgeable.

This understanding of authority must be distinguished from the idea of *auctoritas*, which is likewise located in pagan antiquity but situated in a political context. For example, where Roman constitutional history speaks of the *auctoritas patrum* (authority of the fathers), this describes the "patristic senate faction's [originally the wholly patristic senate's] granting of full speaking rights on legislative acts of the plenary sessions and on the elections held by the higher magistrates," in addition to "full senate resolutions on tribunal and legislative proposals as well as resolutions on war and peace."[3] Authority in this sense, then, refers to the power to enact laws or legal judgments and to preserve them by issuing juridical rulings.

Legislative and juridical authority of this type is central to ordering a society: by demanding universal obedience to the law, it ensures that all—regardless of personal agreement—are bound by the law. Those who violate a law must then face the consequences set down in the laws themselves in case of their violation. The difference between these two forms of authority—the epistemic and the juridical—is that the first form is aimed at inner agreement, while the second is content with outward obedience. Admittedly, laws are subject to normative claims of justice and must accordingly be subject to political scrutiny as to whether they actually are just. But a law does not actually acquire its legal force from whether all individuals consider it just. In a liberal society, legislators cannot expect the individual to agree with any particular law, only that the individual will follow it, even though that individual as a citizen retains the option—once again codified in law—to advocate for a change in that law. In the case of epistemic authority, the situation is different. Epistemic authority is not aiming for outward obedience, nor does it have instruments for compelling it. It is an aid to cognitive interior processes. Epistemic authority can do nothing except offer itself, justify itself as well as possible by giving reasons, and stand up to testing. If it imposes itself, fails to give reasons for the truth of what it testifies to, or fails some other test, it is in danger of losing its status as authority—a status it has only gained by the approval of those who consider it an authority. In short, while a juridical authority can decree and ensure compliance with its decrees through its own authority, an epistemic authority can only advocate for the recognition of what it deems decreed and thus testifies to.

Both of these meanings of authority have a certain degree of legitimacy in Christian theology. God, and only he, is the *auctor* of the world, bringing everything into existence through his creative power. But the God of Jesus Christ is not one who compels recognition of his own authority. Instead he tries to win acceptance through testimony. Especially in the works of John and Luke, the category of testimony—and thus the concept of epistemic authority—is of vital christological and ecclesiological relevance. In the Gospel of John, Jesus says of himself, "For this I was born, and for this I came into the world, to testify to the truth" (John 18:37). He does so by testifying to what he has seen in presence of the Father (John 8:38) and been told by the Father (John 12:50).

The testimony of Jesus, in turn, is attested by people (such as John the Baptist), by Jesus's works, and by Scripture (John 5:32–39). In Johannine theology, the works of Jesus are admittedly performed on the authority of the Father (John 5:27) and are thus an expression of God's authorial action, but their purpose is to become *semeia*, signs legible in faith. This is a concept important in John and, in the form of a seven-sign cycle (John 2:3—11:3) was likely taken from an independent literary source—the so-called *semeia* source, which John adapted and integrated into his work.[4]

Luke is interested less in Jesus as testifying to the Father than in the disciples' role as testifiers to Jesus. To Luke, the preeminent testimony comes from the apostles who experienced Jesus's actions from his baptism to his death and can also testify to his resurrection (Acts 1:21–22). Not only the apostles—whom Luke identifies with the Twelve disciples—but also other members of the early congregation, such as Stephen (Acts 22:20) and Paul, are referred to as testifying, though the latter never knew the historical Jesus but was called to testify only by the resurrected Jesus (Acts 22:15).

The primary task of the Church is to serve through the *martyria* as an epistemic authority testifying to the workings of God in and through Jesus Christ. From the many ways that a life could be lived, those following Jesus choose the "life of faith and charity" as a reality.[5] They can do no more than hope that their actions or their reasons for those actions will convince others. This seems to be precisely what Pope Gregory the Great had in mind when he wrote that the Church arose from a *magisterium humilitatis*, a magisterium of humility, and therefore would "not dictate [to those it deemed erring] from a position of authority, but convince [them] through reason."[6]

The fact that in theological matters of faith the Church is accorded only a testifying, intermediary role in the form of epistemic authority, however, does not mean that there must never be juridical authority within the Church. Indeed, as long as it remains within its bounds, juridical authority is necessary—regarding both its external order as well as its inner confessional structures. For example, there must be binding rules on how to deal with transgressions within the social space of the congregation. There must also be rules for how a liturgy should be held or what procedural pathways must be followed in decision-making. All this requires a legislative competence that can compel members of clergy and congregation alike to follow the laws. But since the faith can never be the possession of one Christian alone—in other words, faith is constituted communally, and being a Christian is inconceivable without some relationship to the larger community of Christians, however that relationship may be determined[7]—there must also be some limited juridical authority in questions of faith. Such a bindingly ordering, decision-making institution is required for testimony to be professed communally, so that testimony of faith can become a confession of faith. The juridical institution, then, is in the service of *homologia*, of joint profession.[8]

In the course of its modernization, however, the magisterium of the Catholic Church has overplayed this hand by—as described above—taking its fundamental task of bindingly testifying to faith and extending this task into categories of Canon law. In so doing, it has categorized its testimony as part of its juridical competencies, while at the same time trying to conceive of those competencies primarily from the perspective of papal sovereignty, which sovereignty consists precisely in not being bound by the Church's testimony to the faith. The Church's epistemic authority—which is essential to the Christian faith—is being overdetermined by a juridical authority that feels compelled to prove its strength by expressing itself in a language of the ultimate and the finally definitive. The magisterium is thus placing pressure not only on those from whom it demands obedience but also on itself: its own claims to superlative authority create an atmosphere in which mistakes are not tolerated and in which there can therefore be no willingness for self-correction. This becomes clear in the context of the claim to infallibility of teachings concerned with truths that are not themselves revealed but "having a necessary connection" with revelation (at least in the opinion of the magisterium).[9] The 1992 *Catechism* even refers to these as dogmas. This new kind of dogma, which cannot in any strict sense be believed but must simply be held as true—legalistically in the sense of *fides tenenda*—lays claim to the Church's juridical authority on the basis only of the Church itself (or at least no longer of revelation). Because of the apodictic way in which the magisterium issues its decisions on teaching, it has great difficulty in developing a self-critical position in which it does not simply insist on its teaching competency but also recognizes that it must sometimes engage in learning as well. The magisterium—as the *Catechism* helpfully notes— still understands its service to the faith primarily as the defense against a state of the world which it perceives as threatening:

> The mission of the Magisterium is linked to the *definitive* nature of the covenant established by God with his people in Christ. It is this Magisterium's task to preserve God's people from deviations and defections and to guarantee them the *objective* possibility of professing the *true* faith *without error*.[10]

The people of God, then, are perpetually threatened by "deviations and defections" that do not affect the magisterium due to the privileged divine support it receives. It is for this reason that the magisterium, which sees itself as founded in the definitiveness of Christ's salvific work, is capable of objectively, truly, and without error presenting the faith in the form of propositions. It should be self-evident why in such a framework it is difficult to admit one's own mistakes, learn from them, and (where necessary) self-correct: such a course would require the magisterium to admit that it too—like all beings—is not above errors and weakness and that it ought therefore to let itself be tested by the power of its arguments and change its position when it is offered arguments better than its own.

MODES OF DOGMATIC DEVELOPMENT

All the cosmetics of continuity notwithstanding, there are countless reorientations of the Church magisterium. However, the magisterium likes to disguise these fresh starts, so as to preserve the appearance of an objective teaching tradition with no breaks. The following will describe three distinct modes of dogmatic development using examples. As working terms, I will refer to these modes as the mode of self-correction, the mode of oblivis-cation, and the mode of innovation veiling.

Self-Correction

Catholic identity today is linked inextricably with the notion of Church office, that is, with the existence of roles within the Church structure and hierarchy. The earliest Christians, living in imminent expectation of the return of their Lord—Paul was convinced that the day would come within his lifetime (cf. 1 Thess 4:15)—had no need of a role-based structure organized with a view to perpetuation. Wherever such a structure did emerge, as it transpired that the second coming was not to be immediate, the structure first diversified before then becoming once again more unified and adopting cultic/pagan notions that had been foreign to early Christianity. (Such adoption can be termed the sacerdotalization of offices within the Church.)

In the early years after Jesus's death there seem to have been three significant groups within the congregation: the Twelve (Mark 3:14), who according to Luke (Acts 1:15–26) were restored to that number by the election of Matthias; the "pillars" (Gal 2:9), as Paul referred to the group composed of James (the brother of Christ), as well as Peter and John; and finally the "seven" (Acts 6:1–7), whom Luke presents as deacons instituted by the apostles but who were more likely a leadership body of the Greek-speaking Judeo-Christians within the Jerusalem congregation.[11] Later, this came to include people like Paul, who while they never met Jesus in person nevertheless justified their mission with a direct order from the resurrected Christ (Gal 1:10–24). The pseudepigraphical Letter to the Ephesians, likely written in the last third of the first century, speaks of apostles, prophets, evangelists, pastors, and teachers, all of whom jointly enable the congregation's service in ministry (*diakonia*) and building up the Body of Christ (Eph 4:11–12). During this period, it is possible to draw a general if somewhat loose distinction between presbyterian and episcopal models for leadership of a congregation. In presbyterian models, leadership follows the tradition of the synagogues and is held jointly by several elders. The episcopal model borrows its nomenclature from Greek administrative structures and has supervisors (*episkopoi*) as the heads of congregations.[12] Over the course of the second century, both models were synthesized, with the *episkopoi*—the root of the word *bishop*—taking a hierarchically higher role. As can be gleaned from the epistles of Ignatius of Antioch, a single congregation was thereafter led by a single *episkopos*, aided by several subordinate presbyters and deacons, though the precise distribution of tasks and responsibilities within this structure remains obscure.

What is remarkable is that the *espiskopoi* at first made no claim to stand in an apostolic succession that might distinguish them from other offices. Instead, Ignatius of Antioch uses typologies of relationships to construct a hierarchy of offices. He sees the *episkopos* as standing in for God ("the bishop is to preside in the place of God"),[13] and it therefore seems fitting that there should be only one in each congregation. The presbyters, according to Ignatius, "are to function as the council of the Apostles."[14] Therefore the bishop is owed the same submission as is due to God the Father, while the presbyters must be followed as the apostles would be.[15] The close link that Ignatius here draws between the apostles and the office of the presbyters was to change when the concept of a particular apostolic succession of the episcopate arose in the early Church's conflict with Gnosticism. In the face of the Gnostic idea that Christianity held secret teachings accessible only to initiates in arcane spaces, not to the congregation at large, Irenaeus of Lyon developed the notion that if the apostles had indeed received secret teachings from Jesus, they would certainly have passed them on to their successors, the *episkopoi*. So, Irenaeus argued, if the bishops knew nothing of such Gnostic teaching, this must be so not because the bishops were uninitiated, but simply because the Gnostic teachings had no apostolic origins. Irenaeus, however, ascribes this apostolic succession to the presbyters as well as the bishops: both together are successors of the apostles and both receive the *charisma veritatis* (charism of truth).[16] Those who depart from the living apostolic succession embodied in the bishops and presbyters, he states further, should rather be suspected of promulgating false teachings. Unfortunately, this line of argument failed to actually settle the matter that Irenaeus was concerned with, to wit, the effective dispelling of Gnosticism. Gnostics, too, claimed lines of succession supposedly linking them to the apostles. The idea that both sides were trying to bolster—that of a "transpersonal authority of the office"—was neither Christian nor indeed specifically religious in its origins.

> It is evident that the Christians did argue over lines of succession, indicating that many people, not just the friends of Irenaeus, accorded them great significance. Incidentally, such formation of traditions corresponds to the actions of other groups establishing an intellectual community, be they philosophical schools or rabbinical groups. Authority was constituted in large measure by referring back to authoritative beginnings.[17]

Since lines of succession were construed differently even in disagreements among groups of Christians themselves, the question of how to ensure the proper investiture of presbyters and *episkopoi* took on a great importance. It is likely that Christian practice, in the beginning, was modeled on the Hebrew Bible, in which at God's behest Moses invests Joshua, "in whom is the spirit," as his successor by the laying on of hands (Num 27:18) as well as on the Jewish tradition, which had its own ordination ceremony based on the laying on of hands:

> Jewish rabbinical ordination (*semikhah*) held great significance between 70 and 150 AD, after the destruction of the Temple and the end of Judaean government in Jerusalem. The rite had been previously used by

51

Pharisee scribes and rabbis, but in a more or less private context. The teacher ordained his pupil, though the teacher himself had to have been ordained, in order to ensure that tradition was passed on....Ordained rabbinical scholars were viewed as the carriers of tradition. Through ordination, the spirit of wisdom necessary for holding the post was passed on in an unbroken chain from Moses down to the rabbi to be ordained.[18]

The parallels with later developments in the theology of Christian Church offices are striking. There too, the laying on hands that an already-ordained officeholder performed on a new officeholder came to signify the effective passing on of succession. In the early Middle Ages, this ordination practice was extended to include the presentation of the instruments necessary for fulfilling the office or of the insignia due to the office.[19] This presentation came to be the constitutive moment of ordination and thus superseded the laying on of hands. The Council of Basel–Ferrara–Florence (1431–1445) is regarded within the Catholic Church as ecumenical. Speaking anachronistically in the language of current magisterial dogmatics, it therefore exercised the solemn, collegial, and infallible magisterium in its rulings. In the course of negotiations with the Orthodox Churches regarding reunion, the Council made important pronouncements on ecclesiology and sacramental theology.[20] In this latter capacity, the Council names the *sacramentum ordinis* as the sixth of seven sacraments. The matter of this sacrament consists in the presentation of the instruments necessary for fulfilling the office: "Thus the office of the presbyter is transferred by proffering the chalice with wine and the paten with bread; the deaconate indeed by the giving of the book of the gospel; and the subdeaconate indeed by the transfer of the empty chalice with the empty paten placed atop it."[21]

The form of the sacrament consists in the phrase that communicates the meaning behind the transfer of the instruments; in the case of the ordination of priests, for example, this is given as, "Receive the authority to offer up sacrifices for the living and the dead within the Church, in the name of the Father and the Son and the Holy Ghost."[22] The Council's pronouncements on sacramental theology make no mention the office of bishop because the Council presumed that the investment of a bishop constituted not a sacrament in the sense of an *ordinatio* but a consecration (*consecratio*), which was either not a sacrament or at least of dubious sacramentality. For in the course of the sacerdotalization of offices, as first the *episkopoi* (later bishops) and then also the presbyters adopted titles such as *hiereus* (priest) or *mediator* (mediator), which the early Christians had ascribed to Jesus alone and would not have used to describe the heads of their congregations, Christian liturgy became increasingly interpreted in the light of cultic sacrificial services. By the Middle Ages, the celebration of the Eucharist—now understood as an act of sacrifice—had thus gained greater importance relative to other aspects of ecclesiastical life. And since it was the priest who had the authority to consecrate the host—and thereby perform the function deemed essential in the medieval point of view—it was also the priest who became the holder of sacramental church office. The investment of bishops, on the other hand, held no added sacramental value over the ordination of priests.

The Council of Basel–Ferrara–Florence followed these same theological precepts, not even granting the bishop the exclusive right to ordain priests. The bishop, according to the Council, is merely the *minister ordinarius*, the ordinary conferrer of priesthood. The qualification *ordinarius* (ordinary) implies that there must also be an extraordinary conferrer of priesthood.[23] This extraordinary conferrer is the priest himself, who can pass on his sacramental office. The two complementary terms *ordinarius/ extraordinarius* are juridical, not dogmatic. Priests, in principle, are capable of ordaining other priests. Although juridically prevented from doing so under normal circumstances, they can be ordered to. What was laid down by the Council remains true also in current contexts of canon law, such as in the sacrament of confirmation: the bishop is the *minister ordinarius* of the sacrament of confirmation, which means that while he is juridically the first and foremost to do so, he is not dogmatically the only possible official to administer confirmation.[24] In principle, priests are capable of bestowing confirmation, just as they are in principle— *pace* the Council of Basel–Ferrara–Florence—of bestowing all of the sacraments (of which the office of bishop was not one). They do so not through the laying on of hands but through the passing on of instruments, again, with a phrase communicating the meaning of the act. The pronouncement of the Council thus gave the utmost binding force to a centuries-old sacramental practice and theology of Church office. It was to stand unchallenged for the following centuries as well.

In 1947, Pope Pius XII made not just one, but multiple corrections to these rulings in his Apostolic Constitution *Sacramentum Ordinis*.[25] Though Pius does not explicitly address the sacramental nature of episcopal ordination, he nevertheless appears to presuppose it when he writes of "the holy ordination of deacons, presbyters, and bishops"[26]—placing episcopal ordination in a line with the ordination of presbyters and deacons, which are uncontroversially acknowledged as sacraments. Moreover, Pius advances a sacramental interpretation of the term *consecratio*, which does not self-evidently connote a sacrament, by using it as a synonym for *ordinatio*, which does usually have a sacramental meaning, when he writes of "the ordination, or consecration, of a bishop."[27] It is therefore only consistent that in the question of who confers the sacrament of ordination, Pius should make no distinction between an ordinary and extraordinary conferrer of the sacrament but see the bishop as the only conferrer of the sacrament. But the most far-reaching change Pius makes is to the form and matter of the sacrament of ordination. Whereas the Council taught that the matter of the sacrament consisted in the passing on of instruments and the form consisted in the phrase uttered by the conferrer, Pius XII now taught that the matter of the sacrament consisted in the laying on of hands by the ordaining bishop. The form of the sacrament, according to Pius, lay in a particular section of the preface spoken during ordination.

The one and only matter of the holy ordination of deacons, presbyters, and bishops is the laying on of hands; and the likewise one and only form are the words determining the use of this matter, which unequivocally signify the sacramental effect—that is to say, the authority to ordain and the grace of the Holy Spirit—and which are accepted and used as such by the Church. It follows from this that we declare, as in order to put an end to all controversy and block the path to anxieties of conscience we indeed do declare by the power of our Apostolic authority, and state, whatever other legitimate disposition may once have been made, that at least henceforth the passing on of the instruments is not necessary to the valid ordination of a deacon, presbyter, or bishop.[28]

From a Scholastic point of view, Pius XII, then, had changed both components of the sacrament of ordination: its matter as well as its form. In its essence, this change is no less significant than if one were to exchange the bread and wine as the matter of the Eucharist for other foodstuffs and replace the words of institution with some other text. To preclude misunderstanding: there are good reasons for celebrating the Eucharist with bread and wine, just as there were good reasons for returning to prayer and the laying on of hands, the form of ordination described in the Bible and in documents of the early Church. There is no fault to be found with the substance of Pius XII's decision. Nevertheless, the ruling did reveal an aporia within the Church claim to the authority of its magisterium, since two subjects endowed with infallibility—an ecumenical council and the pope—explicitly disagreed on a question that touches on the identity of the Catholic Church, in this case how to properly pass on Church office. Pius XII reacted to this problem in two ways.

In the first place and perhaps surprisingly from today's point of view, he emphasized the dynamic mutability of Church pronouncements: "all know that the Church may also change or abolish what it has determined."[29] This statement is trivial when applied to the *ius mere ecclesiasticum*, that is, the laws the Church gives itself for the sake of its own external order and that it can therefore also adapt. But this is emphatically not the case for the substance of the sacraments. The Church views itself as powerless with regard to the sacraments; over their substance, the Church has *nulla potestas*—no power—because they have been given by Christ himself. Given that the occurrence of a sacrament is defined by the correct use of the form on the proper matter of that sacrament, changing both the matter and form of a sacrament constitutes not merely an external adjustment, but a serious intervention. This is especially true of the sacrament of ordination, since every other sacrament, such as the true celebration of the Eucharist, depends on it. It would seem that the authority of the Church to "change or abolish what it has determined" must extend very far indeed.

Second, to ensure acceptance of this change, Pius XII invested it with the utmost authority. In the Constitution, he declares (*declaramus*), decides (*decernimus*), decrees (*disponimus*), determines (*statuimus*), and institutes (*constituimus*) the change "having called upon the great Light, with the power of our highest Apostolic Authority and in certain knowledge."[30] Many contemporaries considered the Constitution a papal ex cathedra ruling—that is, an infallible instance of the extraordinary magisterium exercised through papal primacy.[31] At the least, it was seen as an infallible ruling of the ordinary magisterium.[32]

This is development of Church teaching through the mode of self-correction: Pius XII is explicitly distinguishing what was once (*aliquando*) taught from that which is valid henceforth (*in posterum*). In principle, then, it is possible for the Church to correct itself even in important questions—for what question in the Church could be more important than that of Church office?

Within the Church, Pius's decision was accepted without noteworthy criticism. His successors have seldom had such good fortune, even when they were instituting significantly milder self-corrections. In 2018, for example, Pope Francis changed the *Catechism of the Catholic Church*'s teaching with reference to the death penalty. Where the 1992 text stated that the temporal power had the right to institute a punishment appropriate to the crime without ruling out the death penalty in more extreme circumstances, it now avows that "the Church teaches, in the light of the Gospel, that 'the death penalty is inadmissible because it is an attack on the inviolability and dignity of the person.'"[33] The justification for this is a process of societal learning and change, which has also led the Church to reconsider its teaching:

> Today, however, there is an increasing awareness that the dignity of the person is not lost even after the commission of very serious crimes. In addition, a new understanding has emerged of the significance of penal sanctions imposed by the state. Lastly, more effective systems of detention have been developed, which ensure the due protection of citizens but, at the same time, do not definitively deprive the guilty of the possibility of redemption.[34]

Much like Pius XII with his juxtaposition of "once" and "henceforth" (*aliquando—in posterum*), Francis sets up an opposition between what "was long considered" true and what should be taught "today" (*diu—hodie*).[35] This is an admittedly significant but, in the light of the status quo, nevertheless comparatively gentle self-correction of Church teaching since the *Catechism* before had not advocated or even vociferously defended the death penalty. The *Catechism* had merely stopped short of fundamentally negating its moral-theological legitimacy in the most extreme cases.

Pope Francis's correction, then, is not nearly as precarious for the stature of the Church magisterium as Pius XII's correction of the theology of the sacraments. And yet Francis was confronted with accusations of heresy. One example is the appeal by *First Things*—an influential American Catholic magazine—to the college of cardinals.[36] In this appeal, a group made up largely of US professors, priests, and writers claims that the cardinals have "a duty seriously binding...before God and before the Church" to urge the pope to "withdraw" the change in the *Catechism* so as "to teach the word of God unadulterated." The group's reasons, which are meant to impose upon the conscience of the cardinals, are weighty: a prohibition of the death penalty, the group alleges, contravenes Scripture. The Bible, in their view, does not portray the death penalty as inherently evil, since, in fact, it has been legitimized and at times even ordered by God himself. According to the group, the magisterium has for two millennia continuously taught the fundamental legitimacy of the death penalty, and "to contradict Scripture and tradition on this point would cast doubt on the credibility of the magisterium in general." The petitioners therefore want to draw attention to the "gravely scandalous situation" into which the pope has supposedly brought the Church. "That the death penalty can be a legitimate means of securing retributive justice is affirmed in" Scripture, "and the Church holds that Scripture cannot teach moral error." They lecture the cardinals that in his "refusal to teach this doctrine," Francis has "brought great confusion…and is already causing many people, both believers and non-believers, to suppose that the Church considers, contrary to the Word of God, that capital punishment is intrinsically evil." The cardinals, the petitioners enjoin, must make clear to the pope "that it is his duty to put an end to this scandal" and withdraw the new paragraph of the *Catechism* in favor of their preferred teaching.

Certainly, Pope Francis's ruling, like any magisterial pronouncement, must stand up to criticism and try to offer counterarguments. But the claim that any self-correction fundamentally "cast[s] doubt on the credibility of the magisterium in general" shows a remarkable measure of historical ignorance. Moreover, it is a sign of an ecclesiology so doctrinally narrow that even Pius XII—who is usually held in high esteem among such circles— would probably have been ashamed.

Obliviscation

Since openly announced self-corrections involve the potential for intraecclesiastical conflict and do no good to the aura of the definitively unalterable that the magisterium likes to assume, the preferred modes of doctrinal development are generally more subtle. One alternative strategy consists in producing doctrinal corrections through purposeful forgetting. This mode of change is here described by the neologism *obliviscation*. The word derives from the Latin verb *oblivisci* (to forget), which, rather cryptically, represents a passive verb form with an active meaning. Forgetting thus contains the implication of passivity, of something slipping unintentionally from recollection, side-by-side with an active implication. For example, just as there can be a consciously motivated politics of remembrance, there can be a consciously motivated politics of forgetting. The same is true for the Church: On the one hand, it has an impressive culture of memorialization, which enshrines daily recollection of the actions of not just the Lord, but people—saints—in the celebration of the liturgy. On the other hand, the Church is also capable of organized forgetting. Examples are its own past failures in social or political contexts—and doctrines later recognized as problematic.

One instance of the latter case is once again offered by Pope Pius XII, or more precisely by the reception of a doctrine he deemed highly significant and proclaimed as highly binding. His successor, John XXIII, occasionally gave the impression that the convening of the Second Vatican Council had been a spontaneous idea occurring to him during or shortly before a conversation with Cardinal Secretary of State Domenico Tardini on January 20, 1959.[37] It is possible that the pope did so to conform to a pneumatological trope that inspirations of the Holy Spirit must involve a certain spontaneity. In any case, it seems that there had already been several conversations prior to January 20 in which John XXIII had weighed the possibility of a council—especially as plans and detailed theological preparations for convening a council had already been made under Pius XII. The idea of concluding the First Vatican Council—which had been adjourned *sine die* in 1870 and never reconvened—was thus already in the air. In the end, however, Pius XII chose not convene an ecumenical council—whether as a new or as conclusion of the old Vatican Council—and instead to use the preparations, which he had ordered but had kept secret, in two significant magisterial rulings in the year 1950: the encyclical *Humani Generis* and dogma of the Marian assumption, which he defined ex cathedra several months later.[38] In *Humani Generis*, Pius extensively criticized trends in contemporary theology and issued numerous denunciations, prohibitions, and prescriptions regarding theology.

Among other topics, these edicts covered the Catholic acceptance (or lack thereof) and theological reception of evolutionary biology. More than ninety years after the first printing of Charles Darwin's *On the Origin of Species*, the pope was still of the opinion that the theory of evolution could by no means be considered established. Quite the contrary, in Pius's view: revelation seemed to him to urge the utmost caution in the adoption of evolutionary theory.[39] Nevertheless—and this must be viewed as something of a milestone—he stated that the magisterium did not fundamentally forbid that biologists or even theologians hold the "opinion" that evolutionary theory was true, "provided that all are prepared to submit to the judgment of the Church" when it finally did rule on the matter.[40] This is indeed a remarkable caveat, given that it seeks to subject scientists and theologians alike, regardless of whether they are Catholic or not, to Church judgment on the truth and limitations of evolutionary theory purely on the argument that the magisterium authentically interprets Scripture and the dogmas of faith.[41] Pius then immediately makes use of this newly claimed right to dictate by presenting evolutionary biologists with two facts (as he thought them to be) that according to the magisterium followed inescapably from faith: creationism (with respect to the soul) and monogenism. Creationism (here a belief on the origin of the soul, not the counter-Darwinist world view) holds that each human soul is created immediately by God; that is, that the human soul can have no evolutionary history but that at most the body is subject to processes of evolution. Catholics in line with the papacy, therefore, must subscribe to the view that God observed the evolution of life up to a point where an animal arose whose body functions corresponded exactly to those of human beings today. God then breathed a human soul into this animal, calling it Adam, and thereby created the first human being through an unbridgeable leap of ensoulment.

Monogenism is the inevitable continuation of a (soul-)creationist view: since in Pius XII's opinion, Adam and Eve were the first human beings by virtue of being the first to have a soul, it is only consistent to assume that all other people must be the biological descendants of this first couple. In this manner, monogenism ensured the biological continuation of the Augustine doctrine of original sin, which in the (Western) Church tradition had been conceived of as committed by Adam and Eve and passed down through procreation to all their descendants.[42] If procreation is the mode by which original sin is handed down and all human beings are marked by original sin, then all human beings, Pius XII concluded, must be the biological children of the original sinners Adam and Eve. Any other idea would run counter to revelation and the "documents of the Teaching Authority [i.e., the magisterium—eds.] of the Church," which laid an all-competent claim to being able to interpret scientific questions.[43]

> The situation here seems in fact to be that a well-founded biological theory—that of polygenism—is rejected on theological/magisterial grounds. This is backed up by a self-assurance ready for theological reasons not just to declare a biological theory wrong but also to state what exactly should have been the results of the relevant biological research, which is monogenism.[44]

In its partial if tenuous recognition of scientific research, this strange papal evolutionary theory, idiosyncratically configured from (soul-)creationism and monogenism, nevertheless represents progress relative to the utter and all-encompassing denunciation of evolutionary biology Pius X had formulated in *Pascendi Dominici Gregis*.[45] But *Humani Generis* also shows plainly that with his highly individual logic developed in 1950— that is, at a time when better knowledge was already available— Pius XII put too great a strain on the magisterial claim to offer authoritative rulings. By presenting with his highest apostolic authority supposed facts that he therefore thought all evolution- ary biologists (and indeed all scientists) must accept as given, Pius XII created an embarrassing situation for the Church. Against his will, he himself offered incontrovertible proof of the fallibility of the magisterium. However highly binding the magis- terium might claim its own rulings to be (consider the encyclical paragraph mentioned above and the discussions on the infallibil- ity of the magisterium in general and of *Humani Generis* in par- ticular), no intellectually honest scientist could any longer take what *Humani Generis* propounded even remotely seriously.

As the popes following Pius XII seem to have reached the same conclusion, monogenism was silently dropped. Karl Rahner placed this development as occurring during the papacy of Paul VI.[46] In the *Catechism of the Catholic Church* from 1992, which made the claim to represent the most current and authori- tative document on Catholic doctrine,[47] there is no mention of monogenism. More astonishingly, the *Catechism* in no way mentions the theory of evolution—neither the term nor what it describes appear anywhere. This is an ambivalent silence: On the one hand, a significant question of contemporary Christian faith and a topic that moves many people even outside special- ist circles of theologians is ignored, to wit, how to reconcile faith in a creator god with the insights of natural sciences. On the other hand, the *Catechism* falls back behind even Pius XII's understanding of the problem. Pius at least recognized that the biological research that had so fundamentally altered society's worldview since the nineteenth century would also have con- sequences for the interpretation of faith. If one considers that moreover the *Catechism* offers thorough treatments of the sto- ries of creation and the fall of humanity, complete with literalist interpretations, it is possible to read the *Catechism* from a cre- ationist (here, anti-Darwinist) perspective. Given certain circles within the Catholic Church, it is likely that this possibility was not wholly unintended by the authors of the *Catechism*. Then again, the silence of the magisterium also indicates a silent aban- donment of all positions. No restrictions or prohibitions on the assessment of evolutionary theory are made, much less is another alternative Catholic evolutionary model proposed in opposition to biology. Nowhere, however, is this self-correction by the magisterium discussed. It appears to be hoped instead that Catholics will be capable of forgetting the falsehoods that the magisterium once bindingly issued.

This results in logical problems. Creationism (again in the sense concerned with the origin of the soul) switches places and remains in the *Catechism* with explicit reference to *Humani Generis* (though no longer in the context of evolution, which is left out in any case) as an expression of being created in the image of God and of God's immediacy.[48] But the absence of monogenism with otherwise unchanged hamartiology raises questions. In Pius XII's view, monogenism was necessary to maintain humankind's universal need to be saved within the paradigm of the doctrine of original sin. Under monogenism, it was reproduction through which original sin was passed down to all humankind— but it is precisely original sin as "transmitted by propagation to all mankind" and humankind's resultant need for salvation the *Catechism* continues to maintain.[49] Are all human beings then descendants of Adam and Eve after all? Or is the doctrine of original sin fully independent of biology? What then is meant by "propagation" if not a biological act, specifically procreation, and why should a fact independent of biology be biologically propagated? Or is the statement that "the transmission of original sin is a mystery that we cannot fully understand" a retreat into mystery, a tacit acknowledgment that one is out of one's depth? In short, monogenism is no longer advanced by the magisterium, but because the other components of the doctrine of original sin have remained unchanged, monogenism's silent departure has left a void that has not yet been filled. Little wonder then that, in the face of their internal inconsistencies alone, hamartiology and soteriology in a framework of original sin are being questioned.[50]

To preserve the illusion of its own lack of error, the magisterium is thus dependent on its listeners' capacity to forget. Metaphorically speaking, Mother Church not only nourishes her children with the milk of insight (1 Cor 3:2), but also offers them a sip of the waters of Lethe, the river of forgetting. It is essential for the magisterium's survival that its listeners accept both what it says and what, in the hope that it shall be forgotten, it purposely no longer says. If one took the magisterium too seriously, it would likely drive one insane. It therefore uses discreetly placed acts of forgetting to ease the load on both itself and those who obey it—in the hope that no one will notice or that one will at least silently let the change pass without fundamentally questioning magisterial authority. It is worth examining what this means for theological practice, particularly given growing complaints that Catholics today have too little knowledge of the *Catechism*. To quote one writer, "The Catechism represents the Church's understanding of itself phrased as FAQ. It is the key to the treasury of its unforgettable memories. Through the Catechism, it becomes possible to properly take in the Church's nature and options. The Catechism is the Church's interpretation of Scripture and offers its hermeneutics...in the form of a standardized inventory of its convictions."[51] The lament over a lack of catechistic knowledge, however, could be answered by asking whether perhaps many people are still members of the Catholic Church precisely because they do not know all that once was and in some cases still is written in the *Catechism*. If they did, they might ask, Where has monogenism gone, and what has happened to it? Was Pius XII wrong? If he was, why does no one say so? And if not, why is the Church keeping the keeping the papally defined truth of monogenism from its members? If the Church erred in the question of monogenism, where else might it have erred—and where might it still be errant?

Incidentally, Pope John Paul II's ruling that women can definitively not be ordained as priests[52] belongs in the exact same formal category as monogenism. It is a teaching related only indirectly to revelation; that is, a Church determination that cannot itself lay claim to having been revealed, but nevertheless claims to be necessarily linked with a revealed truth.[53] A Catholic who knew their *Catechism* might ask, Is the definitive exclusion of women's ordination facing the same fate as monogenism?

Innovation Veiling

While the strategy of obliviscation, or targeted forgetting—illustrated above by the example of monogenism—consists in spreading silence over a doctrine so as to let it be forgotten as unobtrusively as possible, there is also a mode of teaching development that, to borrow the words of Hans Blumenberg, attempts to "re-fill newly vacant positions of answers...whose corresponding questions could not be eliminated."[54] This occurs in the hope that the change in position can be made invisibly and in the end, in the best case, remain unnoticed. In the following, I will speak of "innovation veiling" whenever a position is vociferously advocated by the magisterium without ever mentioning that this position is held only due to a fairly recent auto-corrective act. Discussing this act, however, would require or invite self-criticism the magisterium seeks to avoid.

A prominent example is the Church position on freedom of conscience and freedom of religion. In reference to Immanuel Kant, it has already been mentioned how the Enlightenment brought on a growing awareness that religion was a highly personal matter on which a person could not be spoken for or dictated to by any one—least of all by the state. In legal terms, this insight corresponds to granting freedom of religion in the realm of state law. Phrased as a negative, this means that a person must be free from state compulsion in religious matters; phrased positively, it means that a person has the right to follow a religion in the manner that seems appropriate to them, or to practice no religion at all. This positive formulation of religious freedom has three aspects: in the first place, a person must be free to state their faith and profess it; second, the person must be free to practice the acts of their faith; and finally, the person must be free to gather with others of their faith.[55] Full freedom of religion exists only where there is the freedom to profess any faith (or to deny all faiths), the possibility to participate in services of one's own

religion (as well as the absence of any compulsion to participate in any religious service), and the ability for groups of like-
minded faithful to meet in public space for religious purposes
(which, in turn, implies that all religious criticism can lay equal
claim to the same public space). Such rights are only conceivable
in a state that "distances itself from [taking a stance on] the question of absolute truth."[56] In other words, the state must avoid the
kind of total identification with the truth claims of one religion
that would preclude the truth claims of another. This means
that any religious group that affirms religious freedom must also
consequently affirm that the state ought not to take up its truth
claims—at least not as claims to religious truth.

Such a stance, however, runs counter to the position the Catholic Church held for almost one-and-a-half millennia. In the Gospel of Matthew, Jesus's injunction to "give therefore to the emperor
the things that are the emperor's, and to God the things that are
God's" (Matt 22:21) appears to distinguish between the disciples' duties as members in a political commonwealth and their
duties to God. The implication, put rather anachronistically, is
that the order of civil society is not identical to the order of a
religious group. This idea prompted the French historian Numa
Denis Fustel des Coulanges—in a treatise on the ancient Greek
and Roman states that was later to exert considerable influence
on Émile Durkheim—to advance the thesis that Christianity was
the first religion "not to claim that the law depended upon it."[57]
It had thus, Fustel de Coulanges argued, distinguished between
law and religion, thereby making the functioning of the legal system independent of religious questions. At first glance, patristic
texts seem to confirm this view. For example, Tertullian—who
can certainly not be accused of irenicism, in light of his treatment of those he viewed as heretical or his judgment on Greek
philosophy—states that by both natural and human law, all people had the right to venerate whoever or whatever they saw fit:
"However, it is a fundamental human right, a privilege of nature,
that every man should worship according to his own convictions:
one man's religion neither harms nor helps another man. It is

assuredly no part of religion to compel religion—to which free-will and not force should lead us—the sacrificial victims even being required of a willing mind."[58] Tertullian makes the religious quality of an act dependent upon its voluntary performance. Only those sacrificing with a "willing mind" are actually sacrificing, while "compel[led] religion" was no service at all. But it should be noted that in his use of *religio* here, Tertullian is speaking of the Roman state cult. His strategic interest is in denying the religious nature of compelled acts so as to prevent Christians from being forced to participate in pagan sacrificial rites.[59] Tertullian's advocacy of freedom from compulsion in religious matters, then, occurs from a politically precarious position as a minority.

It is hardly surprising that the arguments of Christian theologians changed as Christianity moved from this dangerous minority position to a first politically strong and then even dominant religious stature within the Roman Empire. Political Augustinism—to use a working term coined by Henri-Xavier Arquillière—accorded the state a place firmly within the mission and salvific service of the Church.[60] By the end of the fifth century at the latest, this view became firmly established in a manner that was to shape the Middle Ages. This occurred when Pope Gregory the Great codified in papal state theory that the duty of the *regnum terrestre*, the earthly power, was to serve the *regnum caeleste*, the heavenly power.[61]

> This already clearly shows a crucial characteristic of this "political Augustinism" as it will come to be fully developed over time: The state is given the function of serving the Church and its salvific service and thus itself becomes an institution with an ultimately spiritual goal. The secular power thus veers into the sacral lane....Gregory, then, is purposely elevating the worldly power. On basis of the integration of worldly rule into the order of salvation, which he himself had postulated, Pope Gregory denied the ruled any right to resistance.[62]

From late antiquity onward, therefore, the Church had very specific expectations of what it considered a good state: such a state had to protect and actively support it in its salvific mission. A state that—to once again quote Dreier—"distances" itself from ecclesiastical claims to truth, thus creating the space for religious freedom of its citizens, could not in the Church's view be a good state.[63] The rights that would have gone hand in hand with such distancing, religious freedom most of all, were roundly rejected on the part of the Church. For this reason, there was significant conflict beginning in the eighteenth century, but especially during the nineteenth, as the European nation-states formed and went through often gradual processes of constitutionalization. In 1791, Pope Pius VI viciously criticized the civil constitution of the French clergy and the human rights proclaimed by the National Assembly. The French National Assembly, he opined, mistakenly assumed that there could be such a thing as a "human right" that guaranteed an individual the freedom to hold their own religious opinions and

> to write and even have printed in the press anything relating to religion. The Assembly has itself declared that these decidedly strange affirmations derive from the equality of men and from natural liberty. But what greater stupidity could be imagined than to hold men equal and free without discriminating on the basis of reason, with which man alone stands provided by nature, and by which he distinguishes himself from animals?[64]

Pius VI is campaigning against two of the central demands of the French Revolution—*liberté* and *égalité*—by making the claim that human rights and the fundamental equality of all humankind is unacceptable from a Catholic point of view. Humankind, Pius argues, is so weakened by sin that it is not capable of freely and autonomously making choices in religious matters, but instead requires the Church and kings, whose legitimacy comes from

God, to guide it. The resulting order brings with it an inequality that, in Pius's view, must simply be accepted.

The magisterial pronouncements of the nineteenth century take much the same line. Pope Gregory XVI referred to human rights as "madness," called freedom of conscience "a pestilential error," and accused those espousing freedom of opinion of doing so "with the greatest impudence."[65] Pope Pius IX appreciated these lines, no doubt penned in a spirit of Christian kindness and thoughtful deliberation, so much that in his encyclical *Quanta Cura*, which precedes the *Syllabus Errorum*, he cited Gregory and solemnly denounced the proposition that "the Church should be separated from the state and the state from the Church."[66] From the papal point of view, then, a good state is one identifying itself with the Catholic Church and advancing Church teaching through its laws and actions.

Such a position, however, could be realized only where there was a Catholic monarch, or at least a majority-Catholic population who were capable of shaping national politics in the interests of the Church. Over the course of the nineteenth century, even in places such as these, this position became increasingly hard to implement. Where a Protestant monarch understood his role similarly but with reference to Protestantism, so that the Catholic majority became disadvantaged, the Catholic Church loudly lamented the absence of religious freedoms. This led to a double standard: where Catholics were in the majority or at least had the option of political dominance, they were enjoined by the magisterium not to offer freedom of conscience. Where they were in the minority, however, the pope demanded freedom of conscience for Catholics and gave them the right to use the political process to gain (their own) religious freedoms.

The Jesuit Carlo Maria Curci described this as the distinction between *thesis* and *hypothesis*. *Thetically*, that is, on the basis of principle, Catholics were not permitted to affirm freedom of conscience. *Hypothetically*, however, wherever they were in the minority, they were allowed to use the rights of a liberal nation-state—rights that in principle were to be condemned—to jockey for a more advantageous position for themselves and the Church.[67] The obvious criticism that this amounted to a double standard was addressed even on the eve of the Second Vatican Council and explicitly affirmed by Cardinal Alfredo Ottaviani, who was secretary of the Supreme Sacred Congregation of the Holy Office during Vatican II and later became the first prefect of the newly founded Congregation for the Doctrine of the Faith. As Ottaviani argued, it was necessary to apply a double standard: one standard for truth (that is, the Catholic Church) and one for falsehood (that is, all other confessions). This was justified, according to Ottaviani, because no rights should be accorded to falsehood over truth.[68] As an entity to be granted protection under state laws, the truth of Church doctrine thus had priority even over individual civil liberties. Even under the pragmatic adaptations of the Church, for example in the face of the wave of democratization that washed over Europe after the Second World War, this fundamental approach did not change.[69]

Only after the Second Vatican Council and Pope John XXIII's careful adjustment in *Pacem in Terris* was there any correction of Church teaching on freedom of conscience and freedom of religion.[70] The Council "declares that the human person has a right to religious freedom" and rejects any external or state compulsion in matters of religion.[71] According to *Dignitatis Humanae*, the fundamental entity that the law must protect is not first and foremost "truth," but rather the dignity of the human being. That human being is nevertheless still obliged to seek the truth according to their conscience, and *Dignitatis Humanae* still locates such truth exclusively in the Church of Jesus Christ—thus not going quite so far as some of the Council's other statements on non-Christian religions. But this obligation to seek the truth is a moral one, not one that can be imposed from the outside.[72] Therefore, the right to freedom of religion "continues to exist even in those who do not live up to their obligation of seeking the truth and adhering to it."[73] This changes what the Church expects from a good state. Where a good state previously had been expected to enforce the truth of Catholic teaching, after the Council, "the protection and promotion of the inviolable rights of man ranks among the essential duties of government."[74] But since this is possible only if the state as such distances itself from religious truth claims (a distancing that need not necessarily go hand in hand with a complete separation of Church and state), such distancing is now explicitly demanded of the state—including in places where Catholicism had previously enjoyed a privileged position:

> If, in view of peculiar circumstances obtaining among peoples, special civil recognition is given to one religious community in the constitutional order of society, it is at the same time imperative that the right of all citizens and religious communities to religious freedom should be recognized and made effective in practice.
>
> Finally, government is to see to it that equality of citizens before the law, which is itself an element of the common good, is never violated, whether openly or covertly, for religious reasons. Nor is there to be discrimination among citizens.
>
> It follows that a wrong is done when government imposes upon its people, by force or fear or other means, the profession or repudiation of any religion, or when it hinders men from joining or leaving a religious community.[75]

These new expectations of the state and its constitution are interdependent with the Church's new description of its changed position within the state. For not only is the Church demanding that the state distance itself from religious (and thus its own) truth claims, but it is actually distancing itself from state order as well:

> Where the principle of religious freedom is not only proclaimed in words or simply incorporated in law but also given sincere and practical application, there the Church succeeds in achieving a stable situation of right as well as of fact and the independence which is necessary for the fulfillment of her divine mission.

This independence is precisely what the authorities of the Church claim in society.[76]

In short, the use of state power for Church purposes, which use had been repeatedly sought in the form of political Augustinism since late antiquity, is now given up, and instead a correction is instituted. But the Council nowhere explicitly mentions this about-face, which, in the words of Ernst-Wolfgang Böckenförde, "moves away from previous teaching not merely in degree, but in principle."[77] This is because such metareflection would have been tantamount to admitting that the magisterium had been utterly wrong on an important question—and had perpetuated this error over a period of almost one and a half thousand years. This would have gravely threatened the authority of the magisterium, which, when it finds itself running out of arguments, is inclined to seek refuge in the claim that the Church cannot over centuries lead its faithful astray on significant matters. In other words, if a doctrine is only proclaimed for long enough, it draws its justification from the very fact that it has been held for so long.[78] If this argument is not to lose its persuasiveness, then new doctrines that diverge from old teaching must be disguised: innovation must be veiled. *Dignitatis Humanae* merely indicates that its teaching is due to a new popular consciousness of humankind's inalienable dignity[79] and "greets with joy [this development] as among the signs of the times."[80] What the Council does not mention is that this consciousness and the signs of the times developed not in and through, but outside and in spite of the Catholic Church. Instead, it bends over backward to assert that while religious freedom and freedom of conscience "are fully known to human reason through centuries of experience," they actually have their "roots in divine revelation."[81] Freedom of religion and conscience, which were achieved in opposition to the Church's role as preserver and interpreter of revelation, are now co-opted by revelation theology.

To be clear, the Council's teaching are groundbreaking and trailblazing for the Catholic Church. Accordingly, it is gratifying that the Church seeks to ground its positive attitude toward democracy and individual civil liberties in an interpretation of revelation.[82] Doing so in an intellectually honest way, however, requires simultaneously offering up self-criticism that indicates all the places where one has not done justice to reason and revelation. Of all the victims who suffered under the lack of freedom of conscience and from the interpretation of the state as secular police arm of the Church (from repression all the way to the killing of heretics) *Dignitatis Humanae* says not a word.[83]

This silence makes it possible to transition seamlessly from a never-acknowledged stance of learning into a self-assured stance of teaching, as became clear especially under Popes John Paul II and Benedict XVI. Pope Benedict, in an address delivered before the German Bundestag in 2011, drew a long and unbroken line attempting to trace democracy, the rule of law, and civil liberties back to the encounter between Christian faith, Stoic philosophy, and the concept of natural law:

> Through this encounter, the juridical culture of the West was born, which was and is of key significance for the juridical culture of mankind. This pre-Christian marriage between law and philosophy opened up the path that led via the Christian Middle Ages and the juridical developments of the Age of Enlightenment all the way to the Declaration of Human Rights and to our German Basic Law of 1949 [translator's note: the German constitution], with which our nation committed itself to "inviolable and inalienable human rights as the foundation of every human community, and of peace and justice in the world."[84]

That the line from Roman law through Christianity and Enlightenment to the Declaration of the Rights of Man and the German constitution has been—to put it mildly—somewhat meandering, and that the Church for the vast majority of its existence has been bitterly opposed to human rights, especially rights such as freedom of religion and freedom of conscience, are facts on which Benedict remains silent. Given this omission, he can then self-confidently claim that the "conviction that there is a Creator God is what gave rise to the idea of human rights, the idea of the equality of all people before the law, the recognition of the inviolability of human dignity in every single person and the awareness of people's responsibility for their actions," and that human rights and attendant concepts can only be understood, respected, and preserved with the notion of a creator in mind.[85] He fails to mention that the notions that the Church newly claims only faith in God can secure were bitterly fought against by that same Church in the name of that same God. Since the magisterium of the Church is the interpreter of this "Creator God" by offering binding readings of what he vouchsafes in nature and revelation, however, the authority of the magisterium in its political significance has been once again secured. But this security is purchased at the price of innovation veiling, through which the magisterium can silently reverse its position while pretending that what it so newly teaches had always been taught.

EPISTEMIC AND
JURIDICAL AUTHORITY II

This chapter began by distinguishing epistemic and juridical authority. While epistemic authority views itself as an institution testifying to something understood or experienced as given, juridical authority is capable of determining something by its own power and to compel the recognition of what it has determined. The preceding sections have suggested how the magisterium of the Catholic Church, in the course of its modernization, has sought to cast itself largely in the categories of juridical authority and within the paradigm of sovereign decision-making capacity. This positioning, however, has downsides. It makes it difficult to cultivate a critical relationship with and transparent processing of the limits of one's own knowledge. Explicitly acknowledged magisterial self-corrections are therefore rare; strategies of obliviscation and attempts at innovation veiling, on the other hand, are frequent. In a secular state, the juridical authority of the Church extends only to those who voluntarily grant it epistemic authority, and this epistemic authority is built on credibility. Since the credibility of a person or institution, however, is proved precisely by how they deal with their own mistakes, it is necessary—in the interests of ecclesiastical authority—to arrive at a different conception of magisterial action.

4

CONCEPTIONS OF REFORM

HOW THE CHURCH FORMS ITSELF I

Reform is probably the theological term with the largest and most detailed bibliography of semasiological probing. This is partly due to the fact that the noun *reform* derives from the Latin *reformatio*, making reflections on the term *reform* inescapable in the dialogue over how to conceive of the itself-prominent word *reformation*.[1] The word is noticeably concerned with the philosophically shaped notion of form. For Aristotle, a form (*morphe*) is the "quintessence of definitiveness," while matter represents the quintessence of definability.[2] Pure matter is therefore that stuff (*hyle*) that is literally unformed and nothing in particular, but rather first requires forming or informing to become—in Aristotle's terminology—a *tode ti*, an identifiable "this one." Only form, by pervading matter, can guarantee the recognizability of that which is, because it is the form that is intelligible and capable of being grasped by the human intellect.

Aristotle's metaphysical reflections can be translated into cultural and social contexts as well. Institutions, for example, have to continually work at their form if they want to survive. They do this work by defining themselves, reproducing these definitions, and thus becoming distinguishable and recognizable in the first place. This is especially true of religious institutions, since it is their task to "transform the outwardly (environment) and inwardly (system) delimitable world into one that is definable,"[3] that is, to transform the unmarked state of the world, which is not definitely any one thing but an unbounded potentiality, into a marked state in which previously undefined possibilities find themselves translated into some few realities.

It is this reduction of complexity that creates meaning. "Meaning imposes a form for experiencing and acting which forces selectivity," in other words, the exclusion of possibilities in favor of realized realities—with unrealized possibilities not disappearing once and for all but rather remaining in memory as what was never realized. Accordingly, meaning can be thought of not only as selection but also

> as simultaneous presentation of the possible and the real; a presentation that displaces anything that is intentionally grasped into the horizon of other and additional possibilities....The world-constituting meaning will point to more possibilities than can be processed in the moment through experiencing or acting. This applies to concrete things and occurrences, to signs and abstracted symbols, to others' opinions and to purposes, but also to negative entities such as deficits, absences, or things left out. In all meaningful experience and action, more is constantly being appresented than can be represented.[4]

Giving oneself true definition as an institution, then, is possible solely by transforming undefined stuff into something definite through a process of forming. This transformation leaves behind a remainder of possibility that stays unrealized but potentially realizable. Thinking about reform is nothing else than thinking about that thin border line between the real and the possible, and implementing a reform means shifting that border by transforming either the once real into the henceforth only possible or the possible into the henceforth real.

The Church, in these terms, could be said to have an outward organizational form and a defined doctrine that—as sketched out above—it has decanted into dogmatic form in the context of modernity. These forms were made definitive by excluding numerous other possibilities, as can be shown in countless instances throughout theological and ecclesiastical history. For example, the question of whether non-Jews could ever be receivers of the gospel, and if so under what circumstances, caused considerable conflict within the early Church and has been answered in different ways at different times. These answers have necessitated several shifts of the boundary between the real and the possible. Initially, the Council of Jerusalem would seem to have found a compromise between those skeptical and those encouraging of a wider mission by declaring that heathens could become Christians if they abstained from consuming meat from idol sacrifices, meat that had been strangled, and blood, as well as from fornication (Acts 15:20). Paul supersedes these decisions by effectively allowing the consumption of meat from idol sacrifices (1 Cor 10:14–33). Peter, on the other hand, is less open and withdraws from meals with non-Jews (Gal 2:11–21). Both Peter and Paul in this context sought to redraw the boundary between the real and the possible in the interest of their ideas. This example also shows that not every reality can be rescinded into the possible, just as a possibility that has once been excluded cannot necessarily be made real under all circumstances. There are likely to be irreversibles. It is not only theologically undesirable to turn back the clock on mission and revert the Church to an exclusively Judeo-Christian community, but also factually impossible to do so even if one wanted to.

This is less self-evident in other questions. There are at least three modes available for redrawing the boundary lines between the possible and the real: explicit self-correction, strategies of obliviscation, and innovation veiling. It has been laid out above how these can be used to retransform the formerly real but now only possible once again into the real (the example of sacramental theology); to give up what was once claimed as real once it has turned out to be impossible (the example of monogenism); and to reclaim a first ecclesiastically dismissed possibility as a then later ecclesiastically desired reality (the example of freedom of religion). These developments were possible only because the Church did work on its own form—and thus on its definition— and was willing to reproduce a new definition by adjusting the boundary between the real and the possible. This work on form never ends because at each and every moment, the Church must define itself in its identity as the Church of Jesus Christ. It must do so by embracing the "joys and the hopes, the griefs and the anxieties of the men of this age" as the "joys and hopes, the griefs and anxieties of the followers of Christ."[5]

That is not to say that the boundary between the real and the possible can be arbitrarily and constantly redrawn. It means only that in the face of a heightened awareness of contingency brought on by modernity as discussed in the second chapter, this boundary is no longer generally accepted as self-evident but is subject to argumentative pressures. If this boundary is to be held, it must be held by proving itself meaningful not just through authority but through argument. And if it cannot do so, it must be shifted. It is not enough to look back to the past of the Church and lightly refer to this past as tradition—the prefix *re-* in the word *reform* does not mean a striving for a return to some past ideal or the search for some lost but once extant normative age. Instead, the Latin *reformare* is a loan word for the Greek *mataphorein*, which could be translated as to "change the design of."[6] In the Vulgate, the word occurs only twice, both times in the Pauline corpus. In the Epistle to the Philippians, Paul writes that Christ will transform (*reformabit*) our poor bodies into the shape of his glorified body (Phil 3:21). Here, *reformare* is used to characterize the newly creating, future, and definitive salvific action of God. Paul sees the congregation, too, as capable of creative action, admonishing them in Romans not to "be conformed to this world [here synonymous with the old and the past—M. S.], but be transformed by the renewing of your minds" (*reforma-nimi*, Rom 12:2). The Pauline understanding of reform is thus not one that looks back but one oriented toward the future, challenging the congregation in the here and now. The prefix *re-* identifies not a temporal link back, but an intensified present.

Over the course of later Christian thought, this Pauline closeness between *reformare* and *novitas* has increasingly receded. As the early Church slipped further into the past, it came to be seen increasingly as an ideal to which one must return or against which, at the very least, any theologically desirable state must be measured. Throughout the Middle Ages, this ideal period was increasingly extended to cover the Church of all of antiquity, to which one owed the formulation of central tenets of faith (for example in Christology), but which one simultaneously sought to perceive as unified and harmonious. By ignoring the diversity and conflicts that actually marked the first five centuries, one was thus able to use reference to the Church fathers as a catch-all argument.

> In this constant measuring of one's own time against the yardstick of the past, progress can thus mean only *reformatio* of the old, never *revolutio* or *evolu-tio* of the existing. The ideal state to which one seeks to return is always in the past. *Recreatio, reformatio, regeneratio, reparatio, restauratio, revocatio*—these are the key words which return incessantly and all too clearly. Such a return, significantly, is based not on some general, vague idea of the "good old days" but on a concrete, historically tangible point in time. For all religious reform, this ideal state to be renewed is the Early Church.[7]

Alternatively, the illusory ideal state is the extended idea of the Church in late antiquity, along with its doctrinal achievements. The formula attributed to the Roman bishop Steven I—*nihil innovetur nisi quod traditum est*, nothing must be innovated except for what has been transmitted[8]—became the standard attitude and fundamental theological principle. It has remained so to this day and likely made a considerable contribution to the rarity of explicit self-correction and the frequency of oblivisca-tion and innovation veiling. The last two strategies, after all, have the advantage that one need not acknowledge the novelty of the new.

For example, Pope Francis, by instituting in 2016 a com-mission to study the question of whether in the early centuries women held deacon positions that could be considered sacra-mental by today's standards, is trying to cast light onto a prob-lem that is not without academic interest. But the answer to the problem in no way contributes to a resolution of whether women today could be admitted to Church office, whether as deacons or the full office. The decision of what is theologically justifiable today can never be outsourced to theological history—not even if the commission concludes that the early Church condoned a sacramental deaconate for women. It is asking too much of his-tory and the associated historical disciplines to seek instruction on what to do today or to limit what can be done and believed to what has already been done or believed in the past. Such an approach would imply "that the scope of possibilities in the existing world has already been exhausted; that something truly novel can therefore not arise or be created."[9] Such an assumption is neither empirically compelling nor is there any theologically necessary reason to affirm it.

The consequence is not that the histories of theology or dog-matics become irrelevant—after all, a large part of this book con-sists of historical reflections. But history must not be misused to legitimize. A theological historicization that does not simply lay claim to occurrences for its own ends but rather interrogates the conditions and contexts of the past with a sensitive eye to the chal-lenges of the present will discover just how difficult it is to make historical comparisons and thus draw normative conclusions for current action. "Past thinking becomes less immediately relevant to our actions today the more it is historicized, contextualized, made contingent on the respective culture."[10]

For all that, the Church remains a not merely synchronic but at least as much diachronic community, taking its identity partly from a continuous engagement with the past. But this past cannot in and of itself make normative claims of the present but do so only where it takes the form of tradition. Theologically speaking, however, past and tradition are not identical, which is why the act of transmitting represents not a passive reception of the past but implies a purposeful act of constitution on the part of the receptive subject. None other than Joseph Ratzinger, later Pope Benedict XVI, explained this with admirable clarity: "By self-reflection on the Holy Spirit active within it throughout the tribulations of human history," the Church must ask itself how the encounter with God that occurs in the Church can be conceived of in a theologically adequate way and expressed appropriately in action. "It is this active grappling in the Holy Spirit that is the process of 'tradere'; that is what makes tradition extend beyond Scripture and its letters, not some specific sentence which must be handed down."[11] In other words, the Church receives, constitutes, and reproduces its tradition simultaneously wherever, given its diachronic identity, it confronts its synchronic, present-day challenges and asks how it can be the Church of Jesus Christ living and spreading the gospel today.

CHURCH IDENTITY AND DOCTRINAL CONTINUITY

It is remarkable that in his restructuring of form and matter of the sacrament of ordination, Pope Pius XII managed to perform an act of explicit self-correction in a matter central to Church identity without garnering noteworthy criticism. Pope Francis, in contrast, through his comparatively gentle self-correction with respect to the *Catechism's* moral valuation of the death penalty, was accused of heresy and opened himself up to charges of fundamentally undercutting the credibility of the magisterium and plunging the Church into confusion. It is not too speculative to suppose that had the aforementioned correction of sacramental theology occurred not through Pius XII but through his later successor Francis, its acceptance by today's preservers of the true faith would have been out of the question. This has both subject-specific and independent, more basic reasons. In the development of the magisterium after the Vatican Councils, theological questions on Church office have risen to the level of the sacrosanct, and the liturgy has become an ideological focal point. Furthermore, even those who speak loudly and often of authority have discovered their own antiauthoritarian bent. They follow the pope as long as he happens to be lucky enough to be on their side. These developments reflect a more fundamental narrowing of the discourse: continuity is no longer conceived of primarily in ecclesiastical, but in doctrinal terms. In such a doctrinally narrowed paradigm, the question moves away from whether the Church might not remain true to itself or even better fulfill itself by revealing its magisterium as open to learning and correction. Instead, the doctrinally narrow question becomes what teaching must be preserved in what way and with what degree of bindingness for the Church to remain the Church.

The Second Vatican Council, and Pius XII himself, had a broader understanding of Church identity. However, over the past decades, the question of what the criteria for ecclesiastical self-continuity and thus its continued identity as Church of Jesus Christ should be has been dictated by (and admittedly also partly in opposition to) a small group. Marcel Lefebvre, the archbishop who left his disciples schismatics, is emblematic of the doctrinally narrowed discourse on identity. In his treatise *J'accuse le concile*—a title that refers, with all the subtlety of a wooden mallet, to Emile Zola's intervention in the Dreyfus affair—Lefebvre offers a collection of letters and invectives that include the following:

Because being handed down is in the nature of the Church, it has always had an instinctive revulsion towards renewal, change, and alteration, under whatever pretext: In his encyclical *Mirari vos*, Gregor XVI says: "Since it is certain, to use the words of the Fathers of the Council of Trent, that the Church was instituted by Jesus Christ and His Apostles and that the Holy Spirit through His aid day by day never fails to teach it every truth, it is the height of nonsense and insult to the Church to claim that for the sake of its preservation and progress renewal and rejuvenation had become necessary."[12]

It is true to type that Lefebvre should seek to delegitimize (at least after the fact) a council that pointed out that the Church is "always in need of being purified, always follows the way of penance and renewal."[13] Lefebvre, and all those who did not go as far as he, managed to create a climate in which the discourse on continuity within the Church became anchored to doctrinal narrowing. In this manner, even the smallest changes, such as acknowledging even the possibility of interfaith marriage or allowing (under extremely limited conditions) people living in so-called irregular situations to receive communion, are played up as great breaks of the Church with itself, its tradition, its mission, and finally its God.[14] From the outset, this makes it impossible to have an open and free discussion within the Church on how to position oneself on the urgent questions of our time, such as women's rights, the admissibility for Church office, or the stance on same-sex partnerships. Any time such a discussion looms, the Church's identity—because exclusively doctrinally constructed—appears to be under threat.

This narrowed view is anything but inevitable. Pope Benedict XVI, for example, has distinguished between "a hermeneutic of discontinuity and rupture" and a "hermeneutic of reform."[15] Accordingly the contrast is not, as it is sometimes wrongly presented, between break and continuity, but between "break and rupture," or discontinuity, on the one hand, and "reform" on the other. A "hermeneutic of discontinuity and rupture" with respect to Vatican II, according to Benedict XVI, "risks ending in a split between the pre-conciliar Church and the post-conciliar Church."[16] What this means in practice is exemplified by Lefebvre. To such an approach, Benedict counterposes the "hermeneutic of reform," that is, the "renewal in the continuity of the one subject-Church which the Lord has given to us. She is a subject which increases in time and develops, yet always remaining the same, the one subject of the journeying People of God."[17] What carries continuity in this sense is not dogma as a specifically modern form of representing Church doctrine, but the community of the Church as a subject that develops and cannot be conceived of as fixed if it is to remain itself.

Such an approach, however, raises the question of "whether the form-giving subject can actually guarantee identity without [possessing] diachronic material unity."[18] And indeed, there must be some material specification for where in the Church to locate the question of continuity. The Church is not pure form, but forms a material dictated to it in faith, because its very constitution as Church of Jesus Christ involves at least two materially determinable characteristics. The first may sound trivial: the Church is a *communio personarum*. This is not to set up the term of communion as some preferred category in distinction to other central ecclesiological ideas. The term simply refers to something that—depending on the time and context—might well be described in other metaphors or analogies as well, such as the people of God, the Body of Christ, or simply a society. All these terms, each of which has its own advantages and drawbacks to be discussed elsewhere, have in common that they describe gathering together. The Church, however, is not just any gathering, but—and this is the second characteristic—it views and describes itself as an *ekklesia*, in the language of the Septuagint: as an assembly around the God who seeks communion with it (Deut 4:10; 31:30; Josh 8:35; and more). It is this God that the Church believes to have been incarnated as Jesus of Nazareth and to be present in the Holy Spirit. That is the material identity of the ecclesiastical community that allows it to develop differently, self-critically, even self-correctively over time while still remaining itself.

One of the most incisive explications of this idea, and one whose systematic relevance for the present has not yet been adequately recognized, is found in the writings of Hugh of St. Victor.[19] Hugh distinguishes the act of believing, which he calls *affectus* (not to be misunderstood as referring to any emotional experience), from the propositionally formulated contents of the faith, which he refers to as *cognitio*. "There are two things in which faith consists: cognition and affection, that is, constancy or firmness in believing. It consists in the one, because faith itself is that, it consists in the other, because faith itself is in that. For in affection the substance of faith is found, in cognition the matter."[20] Hugh determines affection to be the nature—the substance—of faith. The contents of faith, that is, the things that are believed, Hugh considers to be the matter of faith and thus that stuff which requires a forming process whose result is termed insight.

By emphasizing that the literally essential part, that is, the substance, of faith consists not of the propositionally definable *cognitio fidei* but of the *affectus fidei*, the faithful turning to God in the community of the Church, Hugh is able to retain a Christian identity that remains true to itself both synchronically and diachronically. Synchronically, both the so-called *simplices* (untutored Christians who are hardly able to speak to the cognitive content of their faith) and the educated who are capable of precisely describing their faith share one and the same faith. Diachronically, both the Christians of Hugh's time and the very first Christians likewise share the same faith, although the doctrines of faith have developed material differences over the centuries.

> This is why, reflecting upon faith, let us confess things more befitting salvation and nearer truth, and just as at one and the same time according to the different capacities of various people we recognize the cognition of those things which pertain to faith, so also let us not

doubt that from the beginning through the succession of the times faith has grown in the faithful themselves by certain increases.

Yet *that the faith of the preceding and the subsequent was one and the same, in whom, however, there was not the same cognition, we thus unhesitatingly confess*, just as in these whom we recognize as faithful in our time we find the same faith and yet not the same cognition of faith. Thus, faith increased in all through the times so that it was greater but was not changed so as to be different.[21]

The ability to see faith (as *affectus*) as unchanging and consistently identical to itself while considering faith (as *cognitio*) capable of temporally contingent change does not fully eradicate the extent to which doctrinal changes and theological self-correction represent threats to Church identity. But it does mitigate them in a way that enables the Church to show a willingness to learn and develop without immediately succumbing to arbitrariness. Strong continuity in the faith exists regarding faith as the turning toward God in the community of the Church. Discontinuities can and are permitted to appear where this faith is laid out reflectively and clarified in propositions.

GOSPEL, CHURCH, AND DOGMA

Clarifying Terms

Since the Church is not pure form but must rather form a material that it is given, this raises the question of how to further define such material—which, in turn, cannot be done without forming it. It is astonishing that little, indeed almost nothing, is known about the what the historical Jesus proclaimed. It is likely that the message of the coming kingdom of God, as shown by eschatological signs, was at the center of his proclamation.

It might have begun with Jesus receiving a vision: "I watched Satan fall from heaven like a bolt of lightning" (Luke 10:18). If Satan, the originator of all evil, has already been overcome in heaven, his disempowerment on earth is only a matter of time—God will create fulfilled salvation on earth soon, too. But what is crucial is that God's reign (*basileia*) has already begun in Israel, since Jesus not only proclaimed God's reign but realized it at the point of his coming.[22]

The beginning of God's reign is thus inseparably linked with Jesus, who was not only messenger, but implementer of this reign, or, to put it differently, was capable of being a credible messenger, an apostle (Heb 3:1), because he was able to realize in his person that which he said. To judge by the Pauline corpus, the oldest texts in the New Testament, however, the early Christians showed little interest in Jesus's biography or teachings, but rather saw the insuperable and thus eschatological significance of Jesus in the fact that God raised him from the dead. It was this faith that became the crucial mark of the circle of the disciples.

"Those who believe in Jesus, the 'Christians,' express their identity through their confession that the crucified Jesus was resurrected by God and seen by people."[23] Numerous confessional formulas found and adopted by Paul testify to this, such as the following: "For I handed on to you as of first importance what I in turn had received: that Christ died for our sins in accordance with the scriptures, and that he was buried, and that he was raised on the third day in accordance with the scriptures, and that he appeared to Cephas, then to the twelve" (1 Cor 15:3–5). The foundation of the Christian faith, then, is not a doctrinal catalog traceable back to Jesus (collections of sayings did exist, but these were adapted only later), but the conviction that God demonstrated his power in Jesus by resurrecting him from the dead. What is foregrounded is God's salvific action as it came to its definitive historical representation in Jesus Christ.

The Pauline writings illustrate how the early Christians summarized this salvific action in a theological reflective term:

the term *gospel*, or *good news*, which Jesus likely did not himself use but was later attributed to him in the composition of the Gospels (e.g., Mark 1:15).[24] The word *gospel* (*evangelion*) was already in pagan usage to describe political messages of success or news of battle victories, but is also documented in the Septuagint:

> The spirit of the Lord God is upon me,
> because the Lord has anointed me;
> he has sent me to bring good news to the oppressed,
> to bind up the brokenhearted,
> to proclaim liberty to the captives,
> and release to the prisoners. (Isa 61:1)

Paul, who discovered a preexisting, specifically Christian usage of the term, adopts it not only in an absolute sense, but also with specifying attributes. For example, he speaks of "the gospel of God" (1 Thess 2:2, 8, and 9; Rom 1:1; 15:16) and "God's good news" (2 Cor 11:7), in the sense of a *genitivus auctoris*, indicating God as the author of the good news. It is thus God himself who is at work in the gospel, and his work shows itself in the fact that it is "the gospel of Christ" (1 Thess 3:2; 1 Cor 9:12; Gal 1:7; Phil 1:27) and "the good news of Christ" (2 Cor 2:12; Rom 15:19)—here in the sense of a *genitivus objectivus*, indicating that it is in and through Christ that the God is offering salvation. This salvific act is instantiated in the proclaiming of the gospel, or in other words, the proclamation of the gospel occurs by credibly representing in word and deed what God has done in Jesus. That is why Paul uses *evangelion* as a noun of action as well, seeing himself as "set apart for the gospel" (Rom 1:1), which is literally inhabited by the dynamic to be a *dynamis tou theou*, the "power of God for salvation" (Rom 1:16) of all people. "Humankind has received the task of proclaiming the gospel (Rom 10:13–15). To that extent, it is a weak human word, which gains its power only from the one who acts through it (1 Cor 2:1–5; cf. Gal 4:12–20; 2 Cor 12:7–10)."[25] Putting the gospel into word and deed thus remains open to human thinking and thus to the human proneness to error.

Dogma represents a specifically modern form of proposition-ally clarifying the gospel: a form in which the Church tries to use its authority to vouch for the actual truth of an expression of the gospel that is claimed to be true. This creates a tension between dogma and gospel. On the one hand, in order to be understood and thus believed or rejected, the gospel requires propositional clarification (even if this clarification need not take dogmatic form). Without such clarification, the gospel would remain unin-telligible and thus could not be believed. On the other hand, the gospel itself is characterized by a surplus that, whatever may have been brought into form, always remains merely appresented and thus cannot be in the literal sense informed.

> Just as the gospel cannot be historically severed from the process of handing down, it is not dogmatically identical to the process of handing down. Rather, the gospel is the power of the uplifted Lord in and above the Church through his living word. The gospel is thus not a historical entity but a present power which con-stantly finds new expression for itself in confession and testimony of the Church without ever being fulfilled in this confession.[26]

Gospel and dogma are both relational and dissociative with respect to one another: they refer to one another and are never-theless distinct. Relationally, the gospel requires the human word so that human beings can grasp it, just as conversely the Church does justice to its mission only when it accurately represents the gospel. Dissociatively, however, the gospel does not fit fully into dogma, which should prompt the Church to continuously follow up on adapting its access to the gospel.

Dogmatic Corrections

The fact that gospel and dogma must not be wholly separate but can never reach full congruity produces within the Church a dynamic aiming to get to the bottom of "the currently not under-stood through a *better* understanding of handed-down testimony."[27]

That which was believed to have already been understood but has turned out in the course of better understanding to require an overhaul can also, where necessary, be reformulated—and that may go beyond mere words. It is not a matter of expressing the same ideas in ever new words. Rather, the Church's daily dealings with the gospel are a learning process that can unearth new ideas and therefore require corrections to Church teaching where these can no longer credibly be proclaimed as gospel. The development of dogma, therefore, should not be understood as a persistent process of addition or as growth in the number of dogmatic propositions. Rather it includes the correction of previous dogma. The Church's persistent work on its form also aims to reform what has already been dogmatically formulated. Walter Kasper pointed this out explicitly:

> Dogma, which in itself ought to serve a love of the Church, may also—through the sinfulness of the actual Church—occasionally transgress against love by being formulated harshly, forbiddingly, with icy rejection, or without understanding for the true petition of the other; by being overbearing or rash in its determination. For the sake of the true function of the dogma, the Church, when it recognizes these defects, could and would have to reformulate its current profession.[28]

Does this now mean that those Church teachings that have turned out to require correction were before simply wrong, and that the Church has taught falsehoods? Depending on the nature of the correction, the answer is yes and no. Moral theology distinguishes between so-called pure and hybrid norms. A pure norm is one consisting entirely and exclusively of "a moral value judgment," while a hybrid norm results from "the linking of a moral value judgment with a judgment of fact."[29] This distinction can be applied to dogmatics as well. There are rulings of faith that can be considered pure in the sense described, such as the profession of God as the Creator of the world. These rulings are in the strict sense neither provable nor falsifiable. In their generality, they are not even bound to any specific cosmology: no matter what else astrophysics may discover about parallel universes or the expansion of space, Christians will always profess God as the Creator of all being, though the way in which God can be conceived of as Creator may change. It is hardly imaginable that the Church could someday conclude that the world as quintessence of all that is was not created by God after all.

However, most rulings of faith are not pure, but hybrid, meaning that they are linked to some factual judgment. This pertains, for example, when the belief in God as Creator finds itself bound up with a particular theory on the origins of the cosmos or humankind. Such theories can indeed be right or wrong. Consider the above example: Pius XII felt compelled to found creation doctrine, anthropology, hamartiology, and soteriology on a judgment of fact—in this case, on monogenism. But monogenism turned out to be simply wrong, and, in truth, always was, because it never corresponded to the real facts of the matter. In this question, then, Pius XII taught something that was false and remained untenable after the error was recognized. Pius's teaching was therefore subsequently abandoned (albeit silently). The need for such correction is obvious in those cases where for example the natural sciences have removed, beyond reasonable doubt, the factual basis for what had been dogmatically determined. In such situations, the Church has the choice of either believing against its better knowledge—thus turning "faith" into simply "not wanting to know"—or else reformulating faith so that it is once more in harmony with knowledge and can once again become gospel to the knowledgeable as well.

Insights from the natural sciences are not the only things that can necessitate dogmatic correction. Deeper theological insights can do so as well—for at the center of what the Church proclaims there is a God who seeks communion with his creation. God's will to such communion, which will is salvific and comes to the awareness of humankind, is known as revelation. As the Second Vatican Council puts it, "In His goodness and wisdom God chose to reveal Himself and to make known to us the hidden purpose [*sacramentum*] of His will...by which through Christ, the Word made flesh, man might in the Holy Spirit have access to the Father and come to share in the divine nature."[30] The Council here makes use of the term *sacrament* to characterize that part of revelation that is to make humankind a participant and companion (*consors*) in divine nature. A sacrament is an outward sign that contains an inner grace, or to put it differently, an occurrence in which God's healing kindness shows itself. Revelation should be conceived of as sacramental because its nature is precisely not in the spectacularly miraculous with which it has often been narratively associated (consider the many biblical accounts of miracles), but in the sober interpretation of apparently profane historical processes, which from the point of view of faith nevertheless reveal God's salvific action. Wolfhart Pannenberg has termed this indirect revelation.

> God, Pannenberg states, does not reveal himself in unmediated immediacy, but in mediated and indirect ways, to wit, through historical occurrences....God's divinity is mirrored only partially and for a moment in an individual occurrence understood as the historical act of God. Therefore God's actions in history must be reflected upon as a whole before the parts come together as one and the moments converge into a totality of meaning. This reflection can only ever be performed in anticipation of a future yet to come, which [brings with it] the possibility of correction and evolution of prior insights.[31]

What Pannenberg refers to as indirect revelation might, in terms drawn more from the Catholic tradition, be described using the word *sacramentality*: those of God's actions that allow humankind to share in the divine nature take place in occurrences that from the point of view of faith represent signs of God's saving grace.

Revelation understood in this manner reached its zenith in Jesus of Nazareth, because as the "mystery of the incarnate

Word" he has given the divine will to salvation a human, bio-
graphically concrete form in sacrament.[32] The lasting significance of Jesus Christ consists not in any doctrinal set he left
behind that the Church might simply hand down. On the contrary, hardly anything is known about the doctrinal teachings of
the historical Jesus. His significance, then, is that God's being "as
it were 'implemented,' purified, disambiguated" itself in human
life "under the conditions of sin, turpitude, and ambiguity of the
human heart [and]...once again revealed itself at the extreme
point of [his] questioning and alienation from the source, in sin,
death, and hell."[33] The christological peak of the conception of
revelation on which the Church must stand thus admits of dogmatic rulings only as hybrid norms. Precisely because God reveals
himself only in time, they are contaminated with the temporal.
God's salvific will reveals itself only in historical, and thus in culturally encoded, form in a contingent interrelation with human
action: in the face of turpitude and ambiguity, questioning and
alienation, sin and death. For the Church, this means that it has
received no sentences from God granting it insight, but that it
interprets actions in which it deems God to be working according to their significance. "Dogmatics thus becomes a description
of actions, and truth becomes the history of salvation."[34] Consequently, dogmatic theology consists not in the reproduction of
doctrinal inventory but in examining the signs of the times for
how (given current knowledge or changing social roles) that
which once occurred in Jesus can today be proclaimed as gospel.[35]

If a statement of faith can no longer be proclaimed as good
news or can no longer be at least placed in relation to the gospel, then the teaching of the Church must change—even if the
doctrines are ones that have supposedly stood the test of time.
This need not mean that what the Church has taught in the past
suddenly becomes wrong in the way that monogenism is simply
wrong and always has been. Rather, it is conceivable that a teaching might simply no longer communicate what all ecclesiastical
teaching must communicate: the gospel. For example, where

a Church office no longer appears as *ministerium*,[36] that is, as an office of service to the faith of the congregation by offering the sacraments, but instead sanctifies some monarchic or otherwise historically contingent hierarchy, this raises the question of where those people who have different notions of a good and justly structured society are meant to see the gospel in such Church office. In the past, such hierarchy may have been an appropriate way to institute the Church in society (or at least, since we are removed from the context of the past, we are in no position to judge); but for the present it is, to put it mildly, open to discussion. If in that discussion it proves to have no argumentative basis, then it must change.

The challenge, however, is that in most hybrid judgments there is no easily discernible core-shell model in which the normative core of a doctrine, which would be worth preserving, could be precisely distinguished from that doctrine's historically determined and possibly interchangeable shell, which could be discarded. Instead, dogmatic rulings are characterized by blurred edges.[37] Just as the stubborn clinging to outdated doctrine risks making historically contingent principles of the past into absolute rules, so the correction of a doctrine also risks disavowing something that might have lasting legitimacy. In other words, not every reform successfully manages to render the gospel in more contemporary terms. Presumably, this is the purpose of the admonitions, heard so frequently from and within the Church, that one must not go with the times. But the alternative—the petrification of doctrine in order to avoid the presumably malign zeitgeist—would contribute to making the Christian faith a museum piece and run counter to its gospel dynamism in spreading "power of God for salvation to everyone who has faith" (Rom 1:16). John Henry Newman has already pointed out this dilemma, simultaneously delivering an undaunted argument for how to deal with it:

But whatever be the risk of corruption from intercourse with the world around, such a risk must be

encountered if a great idea [i.e., Christianity—M. S.] is
duly to be understood, and much more if it is to be fully
exhibited. It is elicited and expanded by trial, and bat-
tles into perfection and supremacy....In a higher world
it is otherwise, but here below to live is to change, and
to be perfect is to have changed often.[38]

The intimacy Newman envisions between the Christian faith and
its corresponding present is revealed in his use of the word *intercourse*. Such a masterful stylist of English prose would not coin-
cidentally have used a word with so clear a sexual connotation,
for all that the word may mean simply "interaction." To extend
Newman's metaphor, then, there is a real risk that the Church
will lose its innocence (an innocence it has never possessed in
any case) if it adapts its doctrine to the times for the sake of the
gospel.

But this is a risk that must be taken. Such an imperative is fed
not merely by a naive optimism but by a deeply Catholic conviction
in the already-discussed dogmatic indefectibility of the Church—
even in those moments when, through too little or too much
reform, it has strayed off the true path and requires correction.
Following the First Vatican Council, there was much discussion
of the infallibility of rulings that were supposed to be unchange-
able and find themselves expressed in the magisterial aspects of
canon law. A late effect of these considerations is the dogmatic
paralysis affecting the Church today because a crucial element—
which was discussed at the Council and also represents the key to
understanding Vatican I from the perspective of the present—has
been neglected: the idea of the *indefectabilitas ecclesiae*, which
is not identical with the *irreformabilitas sententiarum*. That is,
the indefectible nature of the Church does not guarantee that its
rulings need never be reformed. "Consequently, *infallibilitas* can
neither be simply identified in sentences nor be simply fulfilled in
sentences. Numerous sentences may deceive. This is true of the
sentences of Scripture as much as of the sentences of tradition
and the magisterium."[39] This reading is supported by a *Relatio* of
Vincent Gasser, Bishop of Brixen, who attended the First Vatican

Council.[40] Gasser, who belonged the Council's infallibilist majority and presented the draft of the finally approved schema, made
several significant—and in view of his position also semiofficial—
clarifications that in the history of the Council's reception have
receded into the background somewhat. Gasser argues that even
if the pope, in his ex cathedra rulings, is not bound by the prior
determination of an ecclesiastical consensus, his infallibility in
magisterial matters is not distinct from but rather a concrete
instantiation of the *indefectibilitas* which the Church enjoys as
a whole. The infallibility of the pope, he goes on, is therefore not
absolute: *"nullo in sensu infallibilitas pontificia est absoluta."*[41]
If papal infallibility is not absolute, then it must be conceived of
in relative terms—but relative to what? In the first place, relative
to God, who does not deceive in his loyalty, and second, relative
to the Church, to which God has entrusted the gospel and which
he has, the Church faithfully believes, invested with *indefectibilitas* for the sake of the lasting proclamation of this gospel. God
reveals himself to humankind sacramentally, that is, in historically determined situations, which must each be reformulated in
historically appropriate ways in order to become the gospel for
people of all times. This task of reformulation is incumbent upon
the Church. Dogmas, therefore, are not mechanical, stable determinations, but merely historically contingent attempts at setting
down truth—nothing more.

The notion of defect contained in the idea of *indefectabilitas*
describes some shortcoming that ensures that a thing that should
arise does not arise. If, as Vatican II once again emphasized in
Lumen Gentium, the Church as a whole is indefectible,[42] then this
indefectibility refers not to individual sentences or rulings, however much it may be claimed that they are eternal and removed
from everyday dispute. Rather, it refers to the profession and
the living of Christian faith in the congregation of the Church. In
other words, despite all the errors that persist in the Church and
have even been taught by the magisterium, and despite all the
errors that—given human frailty—we must assume are currently
being taught, the Church cannot according to its own faith (for

what is indefectibility if not a doctrine of faith) be so deficient that none of the gospel would shine through in its testimony and actions. No matter in how deep a crisis the Church may be mired: the gospel is too powerful for the Church to be able to wholly obliterate its heart. This is true even though one occasionally receives the impression that the Church expends great efforts in both actions and teaching to extinguish the gospel. Nevertheless, the faith of the Church challenges it to continuously orient itself toward the gospel, and possibly also to correct itself in matters it had previously proclaimed as highly binding.[43] But that same faith can also offer a confidence that enables self-criticism and a courageous attempt at self-correction.

Prudence in the Face of Irritation, Abstraction, and Reconfiguration

In the area of doctrine, discourse on reform only rarely has to do with necessities or impossibilities in the strict sense. Rather, in between the necessary and the impossible, space for the possible opens up and can be used sensibly. Doing so is not a question of dogmatic pseudo-arithmetic, in which magisterial rulings are assessed according to their bindingness or measured according to their degree of immutability. Instead, it is a question of prudence.

In his *Nicomachean Ethics*, Aristotle distinguishes prudence, or practical knowledge (*phronesis*), from other capacities, such as the knowledge and skill to make a thing (*techne*), knowledge about the nature of things (*episteme*), and knowledge of principles (*nous*). To Aristotle, prudence is marked (anachronistically speaking) by the fact that it is capable of offering orientation within a contingent framework: prudence has to do with matters that are as they are but could be different.[44] Prudence is therefore tasked with mediating between the general and the concrete by considering the general in the light of the concrete and the concrete in the light of the general. Prudence aims primarily at the right action, given that there is usually some room for debate as to what that might be. There is rarely only one right way of acting, but often several possibilities which could be acted on prudently. Applied to theology, this translates to the following: there are some right and wrong statements, but no single necessary form of doctrine. Instead, there is a space of possibility that is shaped differently in different eras and within which the gospel can be clarified. It is a matter of prudence to measure out this "possibility space." Prudence can ask how a lastingly valid and to that extent general principle, which is nevertheless accessible only in the concrete, might be reconcretized in another, more readily understandable form. In other words, the questions of whether gospel and dogma stand in a relationship to one another that can still be justified today and what to do if the relationship is no longer justifiable are questions that call for deliberation with prudence. This deliberation occurs in three phases: irritation, abstraction, and reconfiguration.[45]

1   The first stage is the *irritation* of the old by the new. This irritation does not necessarily take the form of conflict, but simply consists of the awareness that doctrine is faced with some phenomenon that is relevant to it but not contained within it. The changing view of homosexuality that has been shaping Western societies for several years is one illustrative example. After homosexuality was first depathologized and decriminalized—in other words, the inclination was no longer treated as an illness and the act was no longer treated as criminal—same-sex partnerships found first tolerance, then acceptance, and finally treatment as a good to be protected by law in the form of civil unions. Currently, at least in most Western societies, they have come to be viewed as equal to unions between men and women, and indeed as marriages in the strict sense.

The social and legal acceptance of homosexuality as "a normal variant of the human capacity for relationship" raises questions for and of Church doctrine.[46] A remarkable fact, and one so far insufficiently recognized within the Catholic Church, is that the demand that the Church join in the legal, civil, and increasing societal recognition accorded to equal rights for same-sex partners does not actually require the Church to give up on or dispense with anything that is dear or important to it. Quite the contrary: the Church regulates marriage through stewardship without—at least in the Catholic view—actually conveying it itself. (It is the spouses who mutually convey the good of marriage upon one another.) The good of marriage is now seen as so profoundly valuable that even those people who have so far been excluded from it want access to this good. This creates theological irritation because, on the one hand, the development concerns the antiquated doctrine of marriage too closely for the Church to ignore, but on the hand, it cannot be easily adapted into the old doctrine of marriage since that doctrine is based on heterosexuality and focused particularly on procreation.

2. *Abstraction* concerns the conflict of whether the Church should take up such developments positively or distance itself negatively from them. The question boils down to whether what the Church proclaims in historically developed concretizations can be made more abstract in such a way as to cover alternative, previously unconsidered concrete situations as well. One point of view would be that limiting marriage to partners of different sexes represents insufficient abstraction. The decisive factor, in this view, would be not the biological sex of the partner but their will to enter a life-long communion of faith and love—a communion that remains oriented to the welfare of both spouses (not merely to the "good...of society"[47] as defined by biological reproduction) and thus has

101

before God such a value that he makes use of the partnership as a means to salvation. Nothing else is indicated by the Catholic understanding of marriage as a sacrament. For the magisterium of the Catholic Church on the other hand, such an interpretation represents too much abstraction. Marriage, according to the magisterium, has been instituted as a bond between man and woman, and as such, serves not only but primarily the act of reproduction which cannot be legitimately influenced by artificial means. Furthermore, according to the magisterium, homosexual couples are not only incapable of this "natural" act but also, if they express their love sexually, commit a sinful one. Since homosexual acts "are contrary to the natural law,"[48] "homosexual persons are called to chastity."[49] Following the logic of the magisterium, the greatest service the Church could do homosexual people would be to lead them to a perfection manifesting in chastity. These two points of view represent the model case of a conflict of abstraction over how to prudently relate the general to the concrete.

3. Regardless of which position wins out, the result is *reconfiguration*, a newly determined reproduction of the form of Church teaching. In the first case, this is obvious, but even the second position, which apparently seeks to keep everything as it is, would wind up casting dogma into a new form. There are countless negations inherent in any affirmation, though some of these negations may become definitively expressed only when the boundaries of the affirmation start to be questioned. Even if the affirmation itself remains unaffected, the emergence of the negations then yields reform—that is, work on the form of Church doctrine with the aim of redefinition. Even without any outward changes in the

Church's position on marriage and homosexuality, the reaffirmation that marriage is a bond between "a man and a woman"[50] today gains the negative meanings "not between man and man" and "not between woman and woman." In previous centuries, the original statement may have been commonplace and thus not worth deeper interrogation because the alternatives were beyond social imagining. Accordingly, the affirmation was not perceived as a negation. Today, changing circumstances around an unchanging affirmation reveal a negation that, although it was always contained in the affirmation, was never questioned—until it was. If the negation stands up to this questioning, the affirmation may remain. But the now consciously emerging negation effects a defensive redefinition of the form.

The chosen example refers to a topic in which the Church, in the face of developments precipitated outside the realm it officially tolerates, must self-critically interrogate whether its teaching is in line with the gospel. Because what it currently offers same-sex couples is simply: nothing. One can hardly blame homosexual people for turning their backs on such a Church.

But there are also irritations arising from within the Church. Theology and Church are not merely passive recipients of the new, but actively shape contemporary culture in interdependence with what the Council refers to as the "world." This work then affects theology and the Church in turn. The distinction between external criticism, whose yardsticks "lie outside the issue being criticized" and internal criticism, with yardsticks "lying in itself,"[51] cannot be applied to theological and internal Church discourses. Christians are not merely members of the Church, but also members of a society and children of their time, with access to knowledge and standards of rationality that are not exclusively ecclesiastical (which would be unimaginable in any case). There are therefore also no purely intraecclesiastical yardsticks for how in line doctrine is with the gospel.

Doctrine must be accountable in the public sphere of which the Church is a part. This accountability is required all the more because the Church views its doctrine as potentially relevant to, and perhaps even necessary for the salvation of, all people. What the Second Vatican Council says of the "world," specifically that it is in transition "from a rather static concept of reality to a more dynamic, evolutionary one" and therefore facing "a new series of problems, a series as numerous as can be, calling for efforts of analysis and synthesis," applies to the Church as well.[52] In that context, it makes no sense to judge the theological legitimacy of a possible synthesis by the polemical categories of adaption or refusal of the zeitgeist. An adaptation to the zeitgeist (whatever that may mean) is not necessarily bad, just as opposition to the so-called zeitgeist need not be in and of itself good. "Questions of truth are neither questions of adaptation nor questions of refusing adaptation."[53] Rather than retreating into narratives of decay in order to prop up flagging ecclesiastical self-worth, it would be more fruitful to engage with contemporary thought and faithfully orient oneself toward the gospel. If the Church were to take both seriously (the subjunctive is fully intentional), it would not need to fear becoming uncomfortable or losing its rebellious character. The gospel is never merely affirmative, which is also why the Church should not misuse it for ecclesiastical self-affirmation. Today's world ought to contain no dearth of topics on which Christians can raise warning voices from a stance of faith.

HOW THE CHURCH FORMS ITSELF II

The foregoing has, I hope, made clear what is meant by my idea of a new conception of the same Church. Church identity is not determined by holding onto an architecture of teaching placed under a historical preservation order by juridical fiat. Continuity—that is, the state in which the Church today can state that is the same as that of yesterday and in which the Church of tomorrow will, it is hoped, be able to say that it is the same as that of today—is an ecclesiastical, not merely a doctrinal phenomenon. This fact has been forgotten, and as a result of its attendant narrow modernization, the Church finds itself in a self-imposed dogmatic bind. In a material sense—or in modern terms, in a dogmatic sense—the Church as community is constituted by its faith that God is revealed in Jesus Christ and made present in the Holy Spirit. It can do justice to its mission only by continuously forming itself according to the gospel. That is to say that it must determine its own form based on the question of how it can credibly proclaim "the power of God for salvation" (Rom 1:16) in word and deed. If the Church recognizes that its past determinations no longer correspond to the gospel as a message that, being for everyone, constantly urges a new present, it must be prepared to correct its dogmas.

This requires due prudence, since—however much it may be a cliche—not everything old is bad, and not everything new is good. The gospel does sometimes require holding on to the old. But there must be an open discussion about whether it does actually require this. The Church cannot escape an argumentative grappling with what the right way might be and what the possibilities actually are. This grappling can no longer be limited to some few clergy such as the Pope or the bishops in a display of sovereign authority. It is a matter for all Christians. And it must be the strength of the speaker's argument, not that speaker's stature in Church hierarchy, that determines the weight given to their words.

5

OUTLOOK

No More Credit

This book began with the Enlightenment, and it shall end there as well. In his rationalist manual of confession, Johann Michael Sailer poses the following question for reformers to ask themselves: "Does my plan keep merely to the outside, or does it actually penetrate into the innermost chamber of the heart?"[1] Probably only God—certainly no theologian—can actually look into the true heart of the Church, into what actually determines the Church according to its innermost nature, into what gives it vitality. Nevertheless, this essay has attempted to show that at least the theologically accessible side of the Church could be conceived of in a different way than it is currently being doctrinally conceived of, and that therefore a discourse on reform need not be satisfied with only surface touch-ups. The calls for reform that seem so tedious to some within the Church do not fit neatly into narratives of supposed nonbelief or growing disenchantment with religion.

On the contrary, all the advocating for reforms within the Church suggests a heightened sensibility for faults and a lively religious interest in their correction.[2] It remains to be seen whether

the Church will, in the future, understand how to adopt and integrate this activity on the part of its members. There are some
signs that changes are indeed possible, especially in the current
pontificate. Other aspects give the impression that the Catholic
Church is taking leave of serious engagement with contemporary
questions and is willing to enrich the present only in the form of
a kind of living museum spread out across the world. In the face
of the reformer as well as the notorious naysayer who believes
that "he need not keep to the usual prescriptions of reason,
because he has received authority from above"—and the Church
has no dearth of such claimants to authority—Sailer offers "but
this word alone: 'Friend! Show us whence your credit.'"[3]

The Church has overextended its line of credit for a certain
mode of being in the world. There are other conceivable forms
of Church being that may make the jump from the possible to
the real, from the conceivable to the actual. This process must
be awaited with skepticism but not without hope, and must be
fought for with strength, but not without love.

NOTES

1. INTRODUCTION

1. Cf. Steffen Martus, *Aufklärung: Das deutsche 18. Jahrhundert: Ein Epochenbild* [Enlightenment: The German eighteenth century; Picture of an epoch] (Berlin: Rowohlt, 2015), 340–41.

2. Immanuel Kant, *Critique of Pure Reason*, trans. Norman Kemp Smith (London: Macmillan, 1929), 652, https://archive.org/details/in.ernet.dli.2015.222508.

3. Johann Michael Sailer, *Vernunftlehre für Menschen wie sie sind, d.i. Anleitung zur Erkenntniß und Liebe der Wahrheit III. Band* [Theory of reason for people as they are, i.e., instruction on insight and love of the truth, vol. 3], 2nd ed. rev. (Munich: Johann Baptist Strobel, 1795), 332, https://www.digitale-sammlungen .de/en/view/bsb10044283. Translated from the German.

4. More than forty years after Sailer's death, his successor Ignatius von Senestrey—bishop of Ratisbon from 1858 to 1906 and one of the First Vatican Council's most influential infallibilists—urged a court of inquisition against Sailer. Senestrey wrote a letter of accusation to Pope Pius IX, in which he first lamented the state of German theology generally before identifying Sailer as the intellectual originator of the problem. For further details on the accusation and its eventual lack of success, see Hubert Wolf, *Johann Michael Sailer: Das postume Inquisitionsverfahren* [Johann Michael Sailer: The posthumous inquisition proceedings] (Paderborn: Schöningh, 2002), 20–33.

5. Sailer, *Vernunftlehre* [Theory of Reason], 331–32. Translated from the German.

6. Friedrich Wilhelm Graf, *Missbrauchte Götter: Zum Menschenbilderstreit in der Moderne* [Misused gods: On the dispute over the human image in modernity] (Munich: C. H. Beck, 2009), 68. Translated from the German. Graf's criticism is directed at religion generally but is exacerbated in the context of decisions of the magisterium, which are nothing other than theology presented with a claim to utmost authority.

2. DOGMA AND ITS PROTECTIONS

1. Walter Kasper, "Dogma unter dem Wort Gottes" [Dogma under the word of God], in Walter Kasper, *Gesammelte Schriften 7: Evangelien und Dogma: Grundlegung der Dogmatik* [Collected writings 7: Gospels and dogma; Foundations of dogmatics] (Freiburg i. B.: Herder, 2015), 58. Emphasis added. Translated from the German.

2. Pope Pius IX, *Dei Filius*, trans. by Henry Edward Manning, https://www.ccel.org/ccel/schaff/creeds2.v.ii.i.html.

3. See Augustin Schmied, "'Schleichende Infallibilisierung': Zur Diskussion um das kirchliche Lehramt" ["Creeping infallibilization": On the discussion surrounding the magisterium of the Church], in *In Christus zum Leben befreit: Festschrift für Bernhard Häring* [In Christ, freed to live: Festschrift for Bernhard Häring], ed. Josef Römelt and Bruno Hidber (Freiburg i. B.: Herder, 1992), 250–74.

4. Until the Second Vatican Council, it was common speak of the bishops "as a whole" as representing the magisterium. An example can be found in Joseph Pohle, *Lehrbuch der Dogmatik* [Textbook of dogmatics], vol. 1, rev. ed. by Michael Gierens (Paderborn: Schöningh, 1936), 56: "The bishops as a whole are infallible, both when in consensus they issue a truth of faith in exercise of their ordinary teaching office (*magisterium ordinarium*) and when in a general Council (*magisterium extraordinarium*) they reach a final and definitively binding ruling on a matter of faith." Translated from the German.

The term *college* with reference to the magisterium of bishops is introduced only in Vatican II. Here, however, it has at least three distinct shades of meaning. While *Lumen Gentium* 19 is purposely careful in noting that the group of apostles is not to be understood as a *collegium* in the strict sense but rather has merely been constituted by Christ *ad modum collegii*, that is, in the manner of a college, paragraph 22 states that Peter and the apostles formed *unum collegium apostolicum*—which accordingly applies equally to the successors of the apostles in conjunction with the successor of Peter.

This clarity is, in turn, contradicted by the *Nota explicativa praevia* on *Lumen Gentium*. The note seeks to ensure that the collegiality of bishops does not limit papal primacy. To that end, it states that the term *college* should not be understood *sensu stricte iuridico* (*Nota explicate praevia* to *Lumen Gentium* 1). It remains open to interpretation whether the negation of *non intelligitur* applies to *sensu stricte* (preserving a juridical significance for the college, if only in a broad sense), or to *iuridico* (meaning that the college is not of a juridical nature at all). In any case, the note specifies that the pope can exercise his authority *ad placitum* (4), that is, as he sees fit, including without the college of which he is the head.

5. An ecumenical and a general council are terminologically indistinct. Today's Catholic Church has come to accept Robert Bellarmine's count of councils. Bellarmine views the general councils of the Middle Ages—which, unlike the provincial synods, occurred under papal approval and reached determinations that applied to the entire Church under papal authority—as ecumenical councils, and thus counts nineteen ecumenical councils from the First Council of Nicaea to the Council of Trent. Within the Middle Ages, however, as exemplified by Pope Eugene IV, a distinction was drawn between a *concilium oecumenicum*, which included representatives of the Eastern Orthodox churches, and a *concilium generale*, which encompassed only representatives of the Western Church.

John of Torquemada offers an interesting suggestion that both seeks to do justice to the schism in the Church by reserving the term *ecumenical council* for unified councils and nevertheless retains the Catholic conviction that the integrity of the one Church of Jesus Christ has been maintained in the Catholic Church in union with the pope. Torquemada distinguishes between a truly universal council, which includes the totality of all bishops of the world (i.e., those of the Eastern Church as well), and a general council *ex parte,* which can likewise have universal significance even if it convenes only a part of the Church, viz. those bishops who stand in union with the pope. For a succinct overview of these questions, see Hermann Josef Sieben, *Kleines Lexikon zur Geschichte der Konzilsidee* [Brief encyclopedia on the concept of the council] (Paderborn: Schöningh, 2018), 36ff.; or for a more extensive treatment, see Hermann Josef Sieben, *Studien zum Ökumenischen Konzil: Definitionen und Begriffe, Tagebücher und Augustinus-Rezeption (Konziliengeschichte B: Untersuchungen)* [Studies on the Ecumenical Council: Definitions and terms, diaries, and Augustine scholarship (Council history B: Research)] (Paderborn: Schöningh, 2010), 107–52.

6. Pius IX, *Dei Filius.*

7. The college's claim to infallibility in its ordinary magisterium extends only to the contents of the consensus determined, not to the correctness of the determination itself. This means, according to Hermann Josef Pottmeyer, that in the case of a "mistaken determination," the pope might well issue a ruling with a claim to infallibility and nevertheless be wrong if the consensus he is supposed to have determined does not actually exist. Pottmeyer therefore concludes that when a teaching of the ordinary magisterium of the college of bishops is presented, it is always "on principle a fallible declaration by the pope that there is an infallible consensus of the [bishops in their] ordinary magisterium." Hermann Josef Pottmeyer, "Auf fehlbare Weise unfehlbar? Zu einer neuen Form päpstlichen Lehrens" [Fallibly infallible? On a new form of papal teaching] *Stimmen der Zeit* 217 (1999): 241ff. Translated from the German.

8. Jean-Michel-Alfred Vacant, *Le magistère ordinaire de l'Eglise et ses organes* [The ordinary magisterium and its bodies] (Paris: Delhomme et Briguet, 1887), 105: "Il y a lieu de distinguer deux sortes de définitions 'ex cathedra': celles qui sont portées par des décrets solennels et celles qui sont portées par le magistère ordinaire quotidien du Souverain Pontife."

9. Pius XII, *Humani Generis* 20, https://www.vatican.va/content/pius-xii/en/encyclicals/documents/hf_p-xii_enc_12081950_humani-generis.html.

10. Cf. Joaquín Salaverri de la Torre, "El valor de las Enciclicas a la luz de la 'Humani generis'" [The significance of the encyclicals in light of *Humani Generis*] *Miscelanea Comillas* 17 (1952): 135–71.

11. Regarding the pope's criticism of approaches he pejoratively termed *theologia nova*, see Pius XII, "Allocutio ad Patres Societatis Iesu in XXIX Congregatione generali electores" [Speech to the Fathers of the Society of Jesus at the 29th general congregation of electors] *Acta Apostolicae Sedis* 38 (1946): 385.

12. The proceedings and affected parties in the context of *nouvelle théologie* are discussed further in Christofer Frey, *Mysterium der Kirche—Öffnung zur Welt: Zwei Aspekte der Erneuerung französischer katholischer Theologie* [Mystery of the Church—opening toward the world: Two aspects in the renewal of French Catholic theology] (Göttingen: Vandenhoeck & Ruprecht, 1969), 102–4. As might be expected, de Lubac felt the conflict as a personal blow. In his meditation on the Church, he reflects that this community has the capacity for "inflicting deep wounds" upon those who are its faithful. These wounds have "no parallel in merely human societies," and indeed the Church magisterium has the "terrifying power" to do things that, outside the context of the Church, one could only consider "utter rape" (Henri de Lubac, *Die Kirche: Eine Betrachtung, übertragen und eingeleitet von Hans Urs von Balthasar* [The Church: A consideration, translated and with an introduction by Hans Urs von Balthasar] (Einsiedeln: Johannes, 2011), 78. Translated from the German.

13. Pope Paul VI, *Humanae Vitae* 16, https://www.vatican.va/content/paul-vi/en/encyclicals/documents/hf_p-vi_enc_25071968_humanae-vitae.html.

14. For a current example of a firm stance that *Humanae Vitae* is infallible, see D. Brian Scarnecchia, *Bioethics, Law and Human Life Issues: A Catholic Perspective on Marriage, Family, Contraception, Abortion, Reproductive Technology, and Death and Dying* (Lanham, MD: Scarecrow, 2010), 248.

15. Josef Maria Reuß, suffragan bishop of Mainz, as quoted in Joachim Schmiedl, "*Humanae vitae* in der Diskussion der Würzburger Synode [*Humanae vitae* in the discussions of the Würzburg Synod]," in Humanae vitae—*die anstößige Enzyklika:*

Eine kritische Würdigung [*Humanae vitae*—the objectionable encyclical: A critical appraisal], ed. Konrad Hilpert and Sigrid Müller (Freiburg i. B.: Herder, 2018), 221–22. Translated from the German.

16. Denis Diderot et al., eds., *Encyclopédie ou dictionnaire raisonné des sciences, des arts et des métiers*, vol. 10, Neufchastel [though published in Paris, the title pages of later volumes indicated Prussian-controlled Neuchâtel in order to evade censors] 1765, 601, https://artflsrv03.uchicago.edu/philologic4/ encyclopedie1117/navigate/10/2544/ and https://artflsrv03 .uchicago.edu/images/encyclopedie//V10/ENC_10-601.jpeg. Translated from the French.

17. Cf. Stephan Dietrich, ed., *Gotthard Wunberg: Jahrhundertwende: Studien zur Literatur der Moderne: Zum 70. Geburtstag des Autors* [Gotthart Wunberg: Turn of the century; Studies on the literature of modernity; For the author's seventieth birthday] (Tübingen: Gunter Narr, 2001), 345.

18. Cf. Detlef Pollack and Gergely Rosta, *Religion in der Moderne: Ein internationaler Vergleich* [Religion in modernity: An international comparison] (Frankfurt a. M.: Campus, 2015), 26–27: "In contrast with philosophical localizations, the sociological considerations of modernity tend to show a greater degree of soberness, though they too are concerned with identifying the place of the modern in the face of radical social, political, and economic change....Unlike discourse in the Enlightenment and Idealism, however, sociological attempts no longer locate the specifically modern in any one principle—liberal subjectivity, say—which in any case derives its fundamental nature only from its societal construction. Sociological approaches thus also no longer feel challenged to unmask such principles. Rather, they identify a plethora of characteristics which they then use to describe modern societies and no single one of which has the significance of an ultimate cause." Translated from the German.

19. Magnus Striet: *Ernstfall Freiheit: Arbeiten an der Schleifung der Bastionen* [The hard case of freedom: Working to raze the fortresses] (Freiburg i. B.: Herder, 2018), 14.

20. In other contexts, Schnädelbach's approach to modernity is decidedly more subtle. Cf., e.g., Herbert Schnädelbach "Gescheiterte Moderne?" [Failed modernity?], in *Zur Rehabili-*

tierung des animal rationale: *Vorträge und Abhandlungen* [On the rehabilitation of the "rational animal": Lectures and treatises], vol. 2 (Frankfurt a. M.: Suhrkamp, 1992), 431–46.

21. Herbert Schnädelbach, "Aufklärung und Religionskritik" [Enlightenment and criticism of religion], in *Religion in der modernen Welt: Vorträge, Abhandlungen, Streitschriften* [Religion in the modern world: Lectures, treatises, polemics] (Frankfurt a. M.: Fischer Taschenbuch, 2009), 27. Translated from the German.

22. Schnädelbach, "Aufklärung und Religionskritik" [Enlightenment and criticism of religion], 28. Translated from the German.

23. That it posits such an inversely proportional relationship is an accusation often leveled at secularization theory, cf. Rodney Stark, "Secularization. R.I.P.," *Journal for the Scientific Study of Religion* 60 (1999): 272: "The secularization theory is as useless as an elevator that only goes down."

24. See e.g., Antje Flüchter, "Der transkulturelle Vergleich zwischen Komparatistik und Transkulturalität" [Transcultural comparisons in between comparative studies and transculturality], in Wolfram Drews and Antje Flüchter et al., *Monarchische Herrschaftsformen der Vormoderne in transkultureller Perspektive* [Transcultural perspectives on monarchic forms of sovereignty in the pre-modern era] (Berlin: de Gruyter, 2015), 2.

25. On the concept of multiple modernities see, e.g., Shmuel Eisenstadt, *Comparative Civilizations and Multiple Modernities*, vol. 1 (Boston: Brill, 2003). Eisenstadt has posited that what starting in the 1950s, modernization theory came to consider the characteristics of (Western) modernity were actually not a coherent whole, but, in fact, also appeared selectively or in combinations different than those prevalent in the West. Therefore, he argued, a multiplicity of modern and nevertheless differently structured societies was conceivable, so that modernity does not represent a global unification movement.

26. For the idea of the mobile category in reference to the Middle Ages, see Kathleen Davis, *Periodization and Sovereignty: How Ideas of Feudalism and Secularization Govern the Politics of Time* (Philadelphia: University of Pennsylvania Press 2008), 5.

27. Volker H. Schmidt, "Globale Moderne: Skizze eines Konzeptualisierungsversuchs" [Global modernity: Sketch of an attempted conceptualization], in *Moderne und Religion: Kontroversen um Modernität und Säkularisierung* [Modernity and religion: Controversies surrounding modernity and secularization], ed. Ulrich Willems et al. (Bielefeld: transcript, 2013), 27–28. Translated from the German. Emphasis in the original.

28. Schmidt, "Globale Moderne" [Global modernity], 28.

29. Jürgen Habermas, "Modernity's Consciousness of Time and Its Need for Self-Reassurance," in Jürgen Habermas, *The Philosophical Discourse of Modernity: Twelve Lectures*, trans. Frederick Lawrence (Malden, MA: Polity, 1990), 2.

30. Jean le Rond d'Alembert, *Essai sur les éléments de philosophie* [Essay on the foundations of philosophy], ed. Richard N. Schwab (1805; repr., Hildesheim: Olm, 2003), 10–11. Translated from the French.

31. Following Habermas's critique of using modernity as a unified analytical category, it nevertheless seems wholly in line with Habermas's thinking to link the dynamic of modernity closely with eighteenth-century enlightenment. Cf. Jürgen Habermas, "Modernity—an Incomplete Project," trans. Seyla Ben-Habib, in *The Anti-aesthetic: Essays on Postmodern Culture*, ed. Hal Foster (Port Townsend, WA: Bay Press, 1983), 3–15.

32. For the following schematic outlines on the Enlightenment period, cf. Michael Seewald, *Theologie aus anthropologischer Ansicht: Der Entwurf Franz Oberthürs (1745–1831) als Beitrag zum dogmatischen Profil der Katholischen Aufklärung* [Theology from an anthropological perspective: Franz Oberthür's (1745–1831) suggestion as a contribution to the Catholic Enlightenment's dogmatic profile] (Innsbruck: Tyrolia, 2016), 44–70.

33. Mr. Boulanger [certainly not Nicolas Antoine Boulanger; more likely Paul Thiry d'Holbach] *Le christianisme dévoilé ou examen des principes et des effets de la religion chrétienne* [Christianity unveiled, or: An examination of the principles and effects of the Christian religion] (London [incorrect claim made to escape censorship, actually published in Nancy]: [no publisher named, again to escape censorship], 1767), 56. Translated from the French: *Ainsi, toutes les religions se disent émanées du ciel; toutes interdisent l'usage de la raison, pour examiner*

leurs titres sacrés; toutes se prétendent vraie, à l'exclusion des autres; toutes menacent du courroux divin ceux qui refuseront de se soumettre à leur autorité; enfin, toutes ont le caractère de la fausseté.

34. Klaus Scholder, "Grundzüge der theologischen Aufklärung in Deutschland" [Basics of the theological Enlightenment in Germany], in *Aufklärung, Absolutismus und Bürgertum in Deutschland* [Enlightenment, absolutism and bourgeouisie in Germany], ed. Franklin Kopitzsch (München: Nymphenburger, 1976), 295. Translated from the German.

35. This is the "religio-philosophical peculiarity of the German in comparison with the French Enlightenment, which was more radical in its criticism of religion," according to Horst Möller, *Vernunft und Kritik. Deutsche Aufklärung im 17. und 18. Jahrhundert* [Reason and criticism: German Enlightenment in the 17th and 18th centuries] (Frankfurt a. M.: Suhrkamp, 1986), 30. Translated from the German.

36. Immanuel Kant, *Critique of Pure Reason*, trans. Norman Kemp Smith (London: Macmillan, 1929), 528, https://archive.org/details/in.ernet.dli.2015.222508.

37. Kant, *Critique of Pure Reason*, 638.

38. Kant, *Critique of Pure Reason*, 639.

39. Kant, *Critique of Pure Reason*, 639.

40. Kant concludes his "Canon of Pure Reason" with the following confession: "Since, therefore, the moral precept is at the same time my maxim (reason prescribing that it should be so), I inevitably believe in the existence of God and in a future life, and I am certain that nothing can shake this belief, since my moral principles would thereby be themselves overthrown, and I cannot disclaim them without becoming abhorrent in my own eyes." *Critique of Pure Reason*, 650.

41. Kant, *Critique of Pure Reason*, 533.

42. Kant explains the term *postulate* as follows: "For the purposes of this enquiry, theoretical knowledge may be defined as knowledge of what *is*, practical knowledge as the representation of what *ought to be*. On this definition, the theoretical employment of reason is that by which I know *a priori* (as necessary) that something is, and the practical by which it is known *a priori* what ought to happen. Now if it is indubitably certain that something is or that

something ought to happen, but this certainty is at the same time only conditional, then a certain determinate condition of it can be absolutely necessary, or can be an optional and contingent presupposition. In the former case the condition is postulated (*per thesin*); in the latter case it is assumed (*per hypothesin*). Now since there are practical laws which are absolutely necessary, that is, the moral laws, it must follow that if these necessarily presuppose the existence of any being as the condition of the possibility of their *obligatory* power, this existence must be *postulated*; and this for the sufficient reason that the conditioned, from which the inference is drawn to this determinate condition, is itself known *a priori* to be absolutely necessary." *Critique of Pure Reason*, 526ff.

43. Jan Rohls, *Protestantische Theologie der Neuzeit, Bd. I: Die Voraussetzungen und das 19. Jahrhundert* [Protestant theology in the modern era, vol. 1: The preconditions and the 19th century] (Tübingen: UTB, 2018), 210. Translated from the German.

44. Augustine, *De vera religione*, in *De doctrina christiana. De vera religione* [On Christian doctrine; On true religion], ed. K. D. Daur and J. Martin (Turnhout: Brepols, 1962), 218ff.

45. On Augustine's use of *cognitio historica*, specifically in reference to interpretation of the Johannine prologue, cf. Augustine, *De trinitate XIII* 1:2 [On the trinity], in *De trinitate libri XV* [The fifteen books of *On the Trinity*], ed. W. J. Mountain and F. Glorie (Turnhout: Brepols, 1968), 382; and Roland Kany, *Augustins Trinitätsdenken. Bilanz, Kritik und Weiterführung der modernen Forschung zu* De trinitate [Augustin's notions of the Trinity: Summary, criticism, and extension of modern scholarship on *De trinitate*] (Tübingen: Mohr Siebeck, 2007), 525.

46. Gotthold Ephraim Lessing, *Über den Beweis des Geistes und der Kraft* [On the proof of the Spirit and the Power] (Braunschweig: [no publisher given] 1777), 9, https://www.digitale-sammlungen.de/en/view/bsb10927792. Translated from the German.

47. Cf. Dominik Burkard, "Schwierigkeiten bei der Beschäftigung mit der päpstlichen Zensur im ausgehenden 18. Jahrhundert: Am Beispiel der 'Causa Isenbiehl'" [Difficulties in examining papal censorship in the late 18th century: Using the example of

the "Isenbiehl case"], in *Verbotene Bücher. Zur Geschichte des Index im 18. und 19. Jahrhundert* [Banned books: On the history of the Index in the 18th and 19th centuries], ed. Hubert Wolf (Paderborn: Schöningh, 2008), 299–316.

48. Johann Lorenz Isenbiehl, *Neuer Versuch über die Weissagung vom Emmanuel* [New essay on the prophecy of Emmanuel] (N. p. or pub., 1778), preface verso 3, https://www.digitale-sammlungen.de/en/view/bsb10411305. Translated from the German. Isenbiehl is here quoting Johann Ernst Faber's translation of a work by Thomas Harmer, *Beobachtungen über den Orient aus Reisebeschreibungen, zur Aufklärung der heiligen Schrift* [Observations on the Orient from travelogues, for the purpose of enlightenment of the Holy Scriptures], vol. 1, trans. and commented by Johann Ernst Faber (Hamburg: Johannes Carl Bohn, 1772), 281, https://www.digitale-sammlungen.de/en/view/bsb11428969.

49. Cf. also the dissemination of papal denunciation in a special edition of a religious journal edited by Hermann Goldhagen: Pope Pius VI, "Verdammung und Verboth des Isenbiehlschen *Versuchs über die Weissagung vom Emmanuel*" [Condemnation and prohibition of Isenbiehl's *Essay on the Prophecy of Emmanuel*], *Religions-Journal*, special ed. (Mainz: Johann Joseph Alef: 1779), https://www.digitale-sammlungen.de/en/view/bsb11113530.

50. Franz Oberthür to Karl Theodor von Dalberg, late 1777 or early 1778, in *Die Passivkorrespondenz Professor Franz Oberthürs* [The letters of Professor Franz Oberthür], vol. 1, ed. Annemarie Lindig (Würzburg, privately printed, 1963), 191.

51. Cf. Marius Reiser, "Die Prinzipien der biblischen Hermeneutik und ihr Wandel unter dem Einfluss der Aufklärung" [The principles of biblical hermeneutics and its transformtion under the influence of the Enlightenment], in Marius Reiser, *Bibelkritik und Auslegung in der Heiligen Schrift: Beiträge zur Geschichte der biblischen Exegese und Hermeneutik* [Bible criticism and interpretation in the Holy Scriptures: Contributions to the history of biblical exegesis and hermeneutics] (Tübingen: Mohr Siebeck, 2007), 219–76.

52. Johann Friedrich Wilhelm Jerusalem to Johann Christoph Gottsched, 12. January 1747, quoted in Karl Aner, "Die

Historia dogmatum des Abtes Jerusalem" [The *historia dogmatum* of Abbot Jerusalem], *Zeitschrift für Kirchengeschichte* 10 (1928): 76.

53. Cf. Johann Friedrich Wilhelm Jerusalem, *Betrachtungen über die vornehmsten Wahrheiten der Religion* [Observations on the most preeminent truths of religion], vol. 1 (Braunschweig: Fürstl. Waisenhaus-Buchandlung, 1785), https://collections .thulb.uni-jena.de/receive/HisBest_cbu_00032740?derivate= HisBest_derivate_00018948.

54. Uwe Schimank, *Die Entscheidungsgesellschaft: Komplexität und Rationalität der Moderne* [The decision society: Complexity and rationality of the modern era] (Wiesbaden: Verlag für Sozialwissenschaften, 2005), 11. Translated from the German. A similar analysis can be found in Walter Reese-Schäfer, *Politische Theorie heute: Neuere Tendenzen und Entwicklungen* [Political theory today: More recent tendencies and developments] (Munich: de Gruyter, 2000), 247ff.

55. Schimank, *Die Entscheidungsgesellschaft*, 47. Translated from the German.

56. Schimank, *Die Entscheidungsgesellschaft*, 46. Translated from the German.

57. Schimank, *Die Entscheidungsgesellschaft*, 73ff. Translated from the German.

58. For criticism of a strict distinction between premodernity and modernity as opposing epochs in the context of decisional action, see Philip Hoffmann-Rehnitz, André Krischer, and Matthias Pohlig, "Entscheiden als Problem der Geschichtswissenschaft" [Decision-making as a problem for the study of history], *Zeitschrift für Historische Forschung* 45 (2018): 254–55.

59. Cf. Eike Wolgast, "Politisches Kalkül und religiöse Entscheidung im Konfessionszeitalter" [Political calculus and religious decisions in the age of religious denominations], *Luther* 76 (2005): 70.

60. Cf. Horst Dreier, *Staat ohne Gott: Religion in der säkulären Moderne* [State without God: Religion in secular modernity] (Munich: C. H. Beck, 2018), 66–71.

61. Immanuel Kant, "Beantwortung der Frage: Was ist Aufklärung?" [Answer to the question: What is enlightenment?]

UTOPIE kreativ 159 (2004): 7–8. (Reprint, translated from the German.)

62. Cf. Barbara Stollberg-Rilinger, "Cultures of Decision-Making" (German Historical Institute, Annual Lecture 2015), London 2015, 6ff.: "Decision-making means: first, isolating explicitly certain alternative courses of action from the infinite, diffuse ocean of the possible, and, second, committing to one of these alternatives, also explicitly, and acting according to it. A decision in this sense is an incision; it creates a caesura in the course of time....A decision is a cut in time. The decision separates the previous from the thereafter—namely the past (in which there were still several options) from the future (in which one has already committed oneself and now acts in accordance with the one option selected)."

63. One could thus describe modernity as "a dynamic which appears to lead to a cultural devaluing of the bindingness of all traditions," at least with respect to their authoritative quality if not necessarily their actual content. Franz Xaver Kaufmann, *Kirche in der ambivalenten Moderne* [The Church in ambivalent modernity] (Freiburg i. B.: Herder, 2012), 47. Translated from the German.

64. Cf. Thomas Gutmann, "Religion und normative Moderne" [Religion and normative modernity], in *Moderne und Religion: Kontroversen um Modernität und Säkularisierung* [Modernity and religion: Controversies surrounding modernity and secularization], ed. Ulrich Willems et al. (Bielefeld: transcript, 2013), 448.

65. Cf. Hans Joas, "Die säkulare Option: Ihr Aufstieg und ihre Folgen" [The secular option: Its rise and consequences] in *Kommunitarismus und Religion* [Communitarianism and religion] *Deutsche Zeitschrift für Philosophie*, ed. Michael Kühnlein, special edition no. 25 (2010): 231–41.

66. Peter L. Berger, *Der Zwang zur Häresie: Religion in der pluralistischen Gesellschaft* [Compelled to heresy: Religion in pluralist society] (Freiburg i. B.: Herder, 1992), 40–41. Translated from the German.

67. Cf. Michael Seewald, "Religiöse Überlieferungen im Zeitalter des 'häretischen Imperativs': Krisenempfindung und Aufbrüche kirchlicher Traditionsdeutung" [Religious transmissions in the age of the "heretical imperative": Feelings of crisis

and new paths in ecclesiastical interpretation of tradition], in *Kirche ohne Jugend: Ist die Glaubensweitergabe am Ende?* [Church without youth: Is the transmission of faith at an end?], ed. Clauß Peter Sajak and Michael Langer (Freiburg i. B.: Herder, 2018), 61ff.

68. Cf. Michael Seewald, "Religion als Kontingenzbewältigung? Präzisierungen zu einem gängigen Topos in Auseinandersetzung mit Niklas Luhmann, Hermann Lübbe und Ernst Tugendhat" [Religion as coping with contingency? Concretizing a common trope through engagement with Niklas Luhmann, Hermann Lübbe, and Ernst Tugendhat] *Jahrbuch für Religionsphilosophie* 15 (2016): 152–79, esp. 163–66.

69. Niklas Luhmann, *Die Religion der Gesellschaft* [Society's religion], ed. André Kieserling (Frankfurt a. M.: Suhrkamp, 2000), 21. Translated from the German.

70. Luhmann, *Die Religion der Gesellschaft* [Society's religion], 141. Translated from the German.

71. The point that even the First Vatican Council cannot be read exclusively as a denial of modernity is made by Hermann Josef Pottmeyer, "Modernisierung in der katholischen Kirche am Beispiel der Kirchenkonzeption des I. und II. Vatikanischen Konzils" [Modernization in the Catholic Chuch using the example of the conception of church in the First and Second Vatican Councils], in *Vatikanum II und Modernisierung: Historische, theologische und soziologische Perspektiven* [Vatican II and modernization: Historical, theological, and sociological perspectives], ed. Franz-Xaver Kaufmann, Arnold Zingerle (Paderborn: Schöningh, 1996), 136ff: "The expansion of a different societal part-system, to wit the sciences with their claim to the autonomy of reason, the Council dealt with in its constitution *Dei Filius*, where it arrived at a recognition of the relative autonomy of scientific reason." Translated from the German. Admittedly, the reason to which Vatican I refers is a *recta ratio*, a "right reason" whose results—such as in questions of the identifiability of God by natural means—have already been predetermined by the perspective of faith (Pope Pius IX, *Dei Filius* 22, https://www.vatican.va/content/pius-ix/la/documents/constitutio-dogmatica-dei-filius-24-aprilis-1870.html).

72. Cf. Hubert Wolf, "'Wahr ist, was gelehrt wird' statt 'Gelehrt wird, was wahr ist'? Zur Erfindung des ordentlichen Lehramts" ["What is taught is true" rather than "What is true is taught"? On the invention of the ordinary magisterium] in *Neutestamentliche Ämtermodelle im Kontext* [Contextualizing New Testament models of office], ed. Thomas Schmeller, Martin Ebner, and Rudolf Hoppe (Freiburg i. B.: Herder, 2010), 236–59.

73. Johann Baptist Hirscher, *Die christliche Moral als Lehre von der Verwirklichung des göttlichen Reiches in der Menschheit* [Christian morality as the teaching of realizing the divine kingdom in humanity], vol. 3 (Tübingen: H. Laupp, 1836), 249. Translated from the German.

74. Joseph Kleutgen, *Die Theologie der Vorzeit* [The theology of prehistory], vol. 1 (Münster: Theissing 1867, first ed. 1853), 98.

75. Cf. Klaus Unterburger, "Internationalisierung von oben, oder: Schleiermacher, Humboldt und Harnack für die katholische Weltkirche? Das päpstliche Lehramt und die katholischen Fakultäten und Universitäten im 20. Jahrhundert" [Internationalization from above, or: Schleiermacher, Humboldt, and Harnack for a Catholic world church? The papal magisterium and the Catholic seminaries and universities in the twentieth century], in *Transnationale Dimensionen wissenschaftlicher Theologie* [Transnational dimensions of scientific theology], ed. Claus Arnold and Johannes Wischmeyer (Göttingen: Vandenhoeck & Ruprecht 2013), 53–68, 62ff.

76. Cf. Franz Diekamp, *Katholische Dogmatik nach den Grundsätzen des heiligen Thomas* [Catholic dogmatics following the principles of St. Thomas], vol. 1 (Münster: Aschendorffsche Verlagsbuchhandlung 1930), 64–65: "Once the magisterium of the Church, in infallible ruling, has issued the teaching, its truth and our duty of faith toward it are now unassailable. Strictly speaking, no further study of the *regulae remotae fidei* of scripture and tradition are necessary to prove the teaching for the faith. Should there be an appropriate result of such investigation, however, it is suitable for increasing the Catholic's joy of faith and for demonstrating to non-Catholics who believe in scripture that it is indeed a divinely revealed truth."

77. *Ipsius Ecclesiae auctoritas in discrimen vocatur.* Pope Pius IX, *Tuas Libenter*, https://www.vatican.va/content/pius-ix/la/documents/epistola-tuas-libenter-21-decembris-1863.html. Translated from the Latin.

78. *Limitanda tamen non esset ad ea, quae expressis, oecumenicorum Conciliorum aut Romanorum Pontificum, huiusque Apostolicae Sedis decretis definita sunt.* Pope Pius IX, *Tuas Libenter*. Translated from the Latin.

79. *Pontificiis Congregationibus.* Pius IX, *Tuas Libenter*.

80. Hermann Josef Pottmeyer, "Modernisierung in der katholischen Kirche" [Modernization in the Catholic Church], 133. Translated from the German.

81. Klaus Schatz, *Vaticanum I: 1869–1870. Band 2: Von der Eröffnung bis zur Konstitution "Dei Filius"* [Vatican I: 1869–1870, vol. 2: From the opening to the constitution "Dei Filius"] (Paderborn: Schöningh, 1993), 174–75. Emphasis: Michael Seewald. Translated from the German.

82. Hermann Josef Pottmeyer, *Unfehlbarkeit und Souveränität: Die päpstliche Unfehlbarkeit im System der ultramontanen Ekklesiologie des 19. Jahrhunderts* [Infallibility and sovereignty: Papal infallibility within the system of nineteenth-century ultramontane ecclesiology] (Mainz: Grünewald, 1975), 353. Translated from the German.

83. Pottmeyer, *Unfehlbarkeit und Souveränität* [Infallibility and sovereignty], 61. Translated from the German.

84. Hermann Josef Pottmeyer, *Die Rolle des Papsttums im dritten Jahrtausend* [The role of the papacy in the third millennium] (Freiburg i. B.: Herder, 1999), 29. Translated from the German. The phrase "from testifier to monarch" is a chapter heading (18), likewise translated from the German.

85. Matthias Joseph Scheeben, *Handbuch der Katholischen Dogmatik: Erstes Buch: Theologische Erkenntnislehre* [Handbook of Catholic dogmatics: First book: Theological epistemology], ed. Martin Grabmann (Freiburg i. B.: Herder, 1948), §464 (218), §493–94 (232–33). Translated from the German.

86. Cf. "De delictis contra fidem et unitatem ecclesiae" [On offenses against the faith and unity of the Church] and "De delictis contra religionem" [On offenses against religion], in

Can. 2314–2319 (*CIC* 1917). For context, cf. Eduard Eichmann, *Lehrbuch des Kirchenrechts auf Grund des Codex Iuris Canonici* [Textbook of Church law, based on the *Code of Canon Law*], vol. 3, rev. Klaus Mörsdorf (Paderborn: Schöningh, 1950), 414–29.

87. Cf. Georg Bier, "Frauen weihen?" [Ordaining women?] *Herder Korrespondenz* 71, no. 8 (2017): 45–47.

88. Pope Paul VI, *Lumen Gentium*, https://www.vatican .va/archive/hist_councils/ii_vatican_council/documents/vat-ii _const_19641121_lumen-gentium_en.html.

89. Pope Paul VI, *Lumen Gentium* 25.

90. See Pope Paul VI, *Lumen Gentium* 10.

91. Pope Paul VI, *Lumen Gentium* 12.

92. Pope Paul VI, *Lumen Gentium* 12.

93. Norbert Lüdecke, *Die Grundnormen des katholischen Lehrrechts in den päpstlichen Gesetzbüchern und neueren Äußerungen* in *päpstlicher Autorität* [The fundamental norms of Catholic magisterial law in papal law books and more recent statements in papal authority] (Würzburg: Echter, 1997), 245. Translated from the German.

94. *Quae in verbo Dei scripto vel tradito continentur.* Pope Pius IX, *Dei Filius*, https://www.vatican.va/content/pius-ix/ la/documents/constitutio-dogmatica-dei-filius-24-aprilis-1870 .html. Translated from the Latin.

95. Cf. Christoph Theobald, "Le développement de la notion des 'Vérités historiquement et logiquement connexes avec la Révélation'" [The development of the idea of "Truths historically and logically linked to the revelation"], *Cristianesimo nella storia* 21 (2000): 37–70.

96. *Acta Synodalia Sacrosancti Concilii Oecumenici Vaticani II (Volumen 1, pars 4: Congregationes generales XXXI–XXXVI)* [Synodal Acts of the Holy Ecumenical Second Vatican Council (vol. 1, part 4: General congregations 31–36)] Vatican City: Typis Polyglottis Vaticanis, 1971), 48 (17–25).

97. Pope Paul VI, *Lumen Gentium* 25.

98. Norbert Lüdecke, "Ein konsequenter Schritt. Kirchenrechtliche Überlegungen zu 'Professio fidei' und Treueeid" [A consistent step: Church law reflection on "Professo fidei" and vow of loyalty], *Herder Korrespondenz* 54, no. 7 (2000): 340.

99. Cf. Peter Hünermann, "Die Herausbildung der Lehre von den definitiv zu haltenden Wahrheiten seit dem zweiten Vatikanischen Konzil" [The development since the Second Vatican Council of teaching on truths to be held definitively], *Cristianesimo nella storia* 21 (2000): 71–101.

100. For the text of the 1989 Profession of Faith and Oath of Fidelity, see https://www.vatican.va/roman_curia/congregations/cfaith/documents/rc_con_cfaith_doc_19880701_professio-fidei_en.html.

101. Pope John Paul II, *Ad Tuendam Fidem*, https://www.vatican.va/roman_curia/congregations/cfaith/documents/rc_con_cfaith_doc_1998_professio-fidei_en.html.

102. *Code of Canon Law*, Canon 1371, https://www.vatican.va/archive/cod-iuris-canonici/eng/documents/cic_lib6-cann1364-1399_en.html#TITLE_II.

103. *Catechism of the Catholic Church* §11, https://www.vatican.va/archive/ENG0015/__P4.HTM.

104. *Catechism of the Catholic Church* §88, https://www.vatican.va/archive/ENG0015/__PM.HTM.

105. Pope John Paul II, *Ad Tuendam Fidem*.

106. Joseph Ratzinger, "Stellungnahme" [Statement of opinion], *Stimmen der Zeit* 217 (1999): 169.

107. Schnädelbach, *Gescheiterte Moderne?* [Failed modernity?] 443. Translated from the German. A similar stance is taken by Ulrich Beck, who interprets antimodernism as a process of religious appropriation of modernity, which process he sees as expressed in conflict. See Ulrich Beck, *Der eigene Gott: Friedensfähigkeit und Gewaltpotential der Religionen* [One's own God: Religions' capabilities for peace and potential for violence] (Frankfurt am Main: Insel Verlag, 2008), 170.

108. Gerhard Ebeling, *Die Geschichtlichkeit der Kirche und ihrer Verkündigung als theologisches Problem* [The historicity of the Church and its preaching as theological problem] (Tübingen: J. C. B. Mohr: 1954), 44. Translated from the German.

3. CHURCH TEACHING AND MAGISTERIAL LEARNING

1. Aristotle, *Topics*, part I, trans. W. A. Pickard-Cambridge, http://classics.mit.edu/Aristotle/topics.html.

2. Colin Guthrie King, "Sokratische Ignoranz und aristotelische Anerkennung: Über den Umgang mit Autorität und Zeugnissen in der antiken Philosophie" [Socratic ignorance and Aristotelian recognition: On dealing with authority and testimony in ancient philosophy], in *Transformationen antiker Wissenschaften* [Transformations of ancient sciences], ed. Georg Toepfer and Hartmut Böhme (Berlin: De Gruyter, 2010), 45.

3. Andreas Graeber, Auctoritas patrum*: Formen und Wege der Senatsherrschaft zwischen Politik und Tradition* [*Auctoritas patrum*: Forms and pathways of senate rule between politics and tradition] (Berlin: Springer, 2001), 1. Translated from the German.

4. Michael Theobald, *Das Evangelium nach Johannes: Kapitel 1—12* [The Gospel according to John: Chapters 1—12] (Regensburg: Friedrich Pustet, 2009), 32—42.

5. Pope Paul VI, *Lumen Gentium* 12.

6. Pope Gregory the Great, "Moralia in Iob VIII 2,3," in *Patrologia Latina* 75, 803C: *Quia vero sancta Ecclesia ex magisterio humilitatis instituta, recta quae errantibus dicit, non quasi ex auctoritate praecipit, sed ex ratione persuadet, bene nunc dicitur: Videte, an mentiar.* Translated from the Latin.

7. Pope Paul VI, *Lumen Gentium* 9.

8. Cf. Walter Kasper, "Dogma unter dem Wort Gottes" [Dogma under the word of God], 77.

9. *Catechism of the Catholic Church* §88.

10. *Catechism of the Catholic Church* §890. Emphasis added.

11. Regarding Church offices in the early Church, cf. Ernst Dassman, *Ämter und Dienste in den frühchristlichen Gemeinden* [Offices and services in early Christian congregations] (Bonn:

Borengässer, 1994), 49–73; Alfons Fürst, "Die Entstehung der kirchlichen Ämter und Strukturen" [The development of Church offices and structures], in *Einführung in die Geschichte des Christentums* [Introduction to the history of Christianity] by Franz Xaver Bischof, Thomas Bremer, Giancarlo Collet, and Alfons Fürst (Freiburg i. B.: Herder, 2012), 385–417; Victor Saxer, "Die Organisation der nachapostolischen Gemeinden (70–180)" [The organization of post-apostolic congregations (70–180)], in *Die Geschichte des Christentums. Bd. I: Die Zeit des Anfangs* [The history of Christianity, vol. 1: The early period], ed. Luce Pietri (Freiburg i. B.: Herder, 2003), 326–36.

12. That this is not a hard-and-fast distinction is shown by the fact that the First Epistle of Clement, with revealing terminology, classes the episcopate as belonging to the presbyters (*presbyteroi*). See St. Clement of Rome, "Epistle to the Corinthians," in *The Epistles of St. Clement of Rome and St. Ignatius of Antioch*, ed. Johannes Quasten and Joseph C. Plumpe, trans. James A. Kleist (New York: Paulist Press, 1946), 25 and 83.

13. Ignatius of Antioch, "Epistle to the Magnesians," in Quasten and Plumpe, *Epistles*, 50.

14. Ignatius of Antioch, "Epistle to the Magnesians," 50.

15. Ignatius of Antioch, "Epistle to the Smyrnaeans," in Quasten and Plumpe, *Epistles*, 67.

16. Irenaeus of Lyon, "Adversus haereses" IV 26,2, in *Patrologia Graeca 7* (Paris: Imprimerie Catholique, 1857 ff.), 1053 C.

17. Hartmut Leppin, *Die frühen Christen: Von den Anfängen bis Konstantin* [The early Christians: From the beginnings to Constantine] (Munich: C. H. Beck, 2018), 190. Translated from the German.

18. Jochen Wagner, *Die Anfänge des Amtes in der Kirche: Presbyter und Episkopen in der frühchristlichen Literatur* [The beginnings of offices in the Church: Presbyters and bishops in early Christian writings] (Tübingen: Narr, 2011), 126–27. Translated from the German.

19. See Arnold Angenendt, *Geschichte der Religiösität im Mittelalter* [History of religiousness in the Middle Ages] (Darmstadt: Wissenschaftliche Buchgesellschaft, 2009), 442.

20. Especially in the wake of Pius XII's corrective rulings, there have been efforts within Catholic theology to soften the

Council's pronouncements on sacramental theology. Michael Schmaus, for example, claims that the Council's stance on form and matter had been nothing more than a "pastoral instruction to the Armenians" (Michael Schmaus, *Katholische Dogmatik 4: Die Lehre von den Sakramenten* [Catholic dogmatics 4: Teachings on the sacraments] (Munich: Max Hueber Verlag, 1957), §281). In the first place, this reading is not supported by the text; second, it runs counter to the recognition within the Catholic Church of the Council as ecumenical and thus as an instance of the exercise of the solemn magisterium; and finally, it stands in conflict with the fact that other rulings of the Council, particularly the maximalist definition of papal primacy (cf. the papal bull *Laetentur Caeli*, www.vatican.va/content/eugenius-iv/la/documents/bulla -laetentur-caeli-6-iulii-1439.html) were not challenged or softened in any such way.

21. *Sicut presbyteratus traditur per calicis cum vino et patene cum pane porrectionem. Diaconatus vero per libri evangeliorum dationem. Subdiaconatus vero per calicis vacui cum patena vacua superposita traditionem.* Pope Eugene IV, *Exultate Deo*, www.vatican.va/content/eugenius-iv/la/documents/ bulla-exultate-deo-22-nov-1439.html. Translated from the Latin.

22. *Accipe potestatem offerendi sacrificium in ecclesia pro vivis et mortuis, in nomine Patris et Filii et Spiritus sancti.* Pope Eugene IV, *Exultate Deo*. Translated from the Latin.

23. The Council's pronouncements on the other sacraments, such as on the Eucharist itself, on penitence, or on extreme unction, lack the qualification *ordinarius*. There, the priest is simply described as the *minister*, the only conferrer of these sacraments. See Pope Eugene IV, *Exultate Deo*.

24. See, e.g., can. 882 (*CIC*).

25. Cf. the commentary by Franz Hürth, which is significant given Hürth's considerable influence in the papacy of Pius XII: Franz Hürth, "Constitutio Apostolica de Sacris Ordinibus Diaconatus, Presbyteratus, Episcopatus. Textus et Commentarius cum Appendice" [Apostolic constitution on the holy ordination of deacons, presbyters, and bishops: Text and commentary including appendices] *Periodica de re morali, canonica, liturgica* 37 (1948): 9–41. Differing appraisals, though nevertheless reliant on Hürth, are given by Bernhard Brinkmann, "Die Apostolische

Konstitution Pius XII. 'Sacramentum Ordinis' vom 30. November 1947" [Pius XII's Apostolic constitution 'Sacramentum Ordinis' of November 30, 1947] *Theologische Quartalsschrift* 130 (1950): 311–36.

26. *Sacra ordinatio diaconatus, presbyteratus et episcopatus*, Pope Pius XII, *Sacramentum Ordinis*, https://www.vatican.va/content/pius-xii/la/apost_constitutions/documents/hf_p-xii_apc_19471130_sacramentum-ordinis.html.

27. *Ordinatione seu consecratione episcopalis*, Pope Pius XII, *Sacramentum ordinis*. Translated from the Latin.

28. *Sacrorum Ordinum Diaconatus, Presbyteratus et Episcopatus materiam eamque unam esse manuum impositionem; formam vero itemque unam esse verba applicationem huius materiae determinantia, quibus univoce significantur effectus sacramentales—scilicet potestas Ordinis et gratia Spiritus Sancti—quaeque ab Ecclesia qua talia accipiuntur et usurpantur. Hinc consequitur ut declaremus, sicut revera ad omnem controversiam auferendam et ad conscientiarum anxietatibus viam praecludendam, Apostolica Nostra Auctoritate declaramus, et, si unquam aliter legitime dispositum fuerit, statuimus instrumentorum traditionem saltem in posterum non esse necessariam ad Sacrorum Diaconatus, Presbyteratus et Episcopatus Ordinum validitatem.* Pope Pius XII, *Sacramentum Ordinis*.

29. *Omnes norunt Ecclesiam quod statuit etiam mutare et abrogare valere.* Pope Pius XII, *Sacramentum Ordinis*.

30. *Divino lumine invocato, suprema Nostra Apostolica Auctoritate et certa scientia.* Pope Pius XII, *Sacramentum Ordinis*.

31. Cf. Brinkmann, "Die Apostolische Konstitution," 333. Brinkmann sees the Pius XII's determinations of the matter and form of the sacrament as a *definito ex cathedra*.

32. Brinkmann later revised his view that the constitution represented an ex cathedra ruling, but continued to maintain that Pius had issued an infallible pronouncement, since, in Brinkmann's view, Pius had determined a consensus among the bishops on this question. Bernhard Brinkmann, "Enthält die Apostolische Konstitution 'Sacramentum Ordinis' Pius' XII. eine Kathedralentscheidung?" [Does Pius XII's apostolic constitution

'Sacramentum Ordinis' contain an ex cathedra ruling?] *Theologische Quartalschrift* 136 (1956): 321–23.

33. *Catechism of the Catholic Church*, 2267, https://www.vatican.va/archive/ENG0015/_INDEX.HTM.

34. *Catechism of the Catholic Church*, 2267.

35. *Catechism of the Catholic Church*, 2267.

36. Hardley Arkes et al., "An Appeal to the Cardinals of the Catholic Church," https://www.firstthings.com/web-exclusives/2018/08/an-appeal-to-the-cardinals-of-the-catholic-church. All subsequent quotations are taken from the article.

37. Otto Hermann Pesch, *Das Zweite Vatikanische Konzil. Vorgeschichte—Verlauf—Ergebnisse—Wirkungsgeschichte* [The Second Vatican Council: Prehistory—course—results—influence] (Kevelaer: Topos, 2012), 43–47.

38. See Peter Pfister, ed., *Eugenio Pacelli—Pius XII (1876–1958) in the Assessment of Scholarship* (Regensburg: Schnell + Steiner, 2009), 41–62.

39. Pope Pius XII, *Humani Generis* 36, https://www.vatican.va/content/pius-xii/en/encyclicals/documents/hf_p-xii_enc_12081950_humani-generis.html.

40. Pope Pius XII, *Humani Generis* 36.

41. Pope Pius XII, *Humani Generis* 36.

42. Pope Pius XII, *Humani Generis* 37.

43. Pope Pius XII, *Humani Generis* 37.

44. Ulrich Lüke, *"Als Anfang schuf Gott…": Bio-Theologie: Zeit—Evolution—Hominisation* ["As a beginning, God created…": Bio-theology; Time—evolution—hominization] (Paderborn: Schöningh, 1997), 256. Translated from the German.

45. On the changing positions of the magisterium with respect to evolutionary theory, see the survey in Wolfgang Beinert and Bertram Stubenrauch, eds., *Neues Lexikon der Dogmatik* [New dictionary of dogmatics] (Freiburg i. B.: Herder, 2012), 206.

46. Karl Rahner, "Naturwissenschaft und vernünftiger Glaube" [Natural science and reasonable faith], in Karl Rahner, *Sämtliche Werke 30: Anstöße systematischer Theologie: Beiträge zur Fundamentaltheologie und Dogmatik* [Complete Works, vol. 30: Impulses in systematic theology; Contributions to fundamental theology and dogmatics] (Freiburg i. B.: Herder, 2009), 420.

47. Pope John Paul II, *Catechesi Tradendae* 50, https://www.vatican.va/content/john-paul-ii/en/apost_exhortations/documents/hf_jp-ii_exh_16101979_catechesi-tradendae.html.

48. *Catechism of the Catholic Church*, 366.

49. *Catechism of the Catholic Church*, 404–5.

50. Cf. Thomas Pröpper, *Theologische Anthropologie* [Theological anthropology], vol. 2 (Freiburg i. B.: Herder, 2011), 1089: "In the face of these findings, which, it must once again be emphasized, result solely from an immanent assessment of the theory of original sin, I fail to see how justifying or further advocating this teaching could still be the task of theology—unless theology, under the guise of mere magisterial obsequity, should seek to divest itself of its specific tasks. Since the doctrine of original sin at this point creates more problems than positive insight and guidance, it is more a burden than a service to the gospel. If I see rightly, however, this summary only expresses what has long been going on: a large-scale departure from classical teaching of the doctrine of original sin, and in particular from its identification of original sin as that punishable fault and *propagatione transfusum* [transmitted by reproduction]. Yet—and it is against this point alone that my criticism is directed—this departure occurs without bidding the doctrine a clear farewell, which in my view would be more honest and is likely also necessary in the face of its deep, lingering effects." Translated from the German.

51. Bernhard Meuser, "Der verlorene Schlüssel: Warum Katechese den Katechismus braucht" [The lost key: Why catechesis requires the Catechism], in *Kirche ohne Jugend: Ist die Glaubensweitergabe am Ende?* [Church without youth: Has the passing down of faith reached its end?], ed. Clauß Peter Sajak and Michael Langer, (Freiburg i. B.: Herder, 2018), 116. Translated from the German.

52. Pope John Paul II, *Ordinatio Sacerdotalis*.

53. Cf. Pottmeyer, "Auf fehlbare Weise unfehlbar?" [Fallibly infallible?], 240.

54. Hans Blumenberg, *Die Legitimität der Neuzeit* [The legitimacy of modernity], rev. ed. (Frankfurt a. M.: Suhrkamp, 2016), 75. Translated from the German.

55. Cf. Dreier, *Staat ohne Gott* [State without God], 94.

56. Dreier, *Staat ohne Gott* [State without God], 9. Translated from the German.

57. Numa Denis Fustel de Coulanges, *La cité antique. Étude sur le culte, le droit, les institutions de la Grèce et de Rome* [The ancient city: Study on the religion, law, and instituations of Greece and Rome] (Paris: Durand, 1864), 520: "Le christianisme est la première religion qui n'ait pas prétendue que le droit dépendît d'elle. Il s'occupa des devoirs des hommes, non de leurs relations d'intérêts."

58. Tertullian, "Ad Scapulam," trans. S. Thelwall, in *The Writings of Quintus Sept. Flor. Tertullianus*, vol. 1 (Edinburgh: T. & T. Clark, 1869), in *Ante-Nicene Christian Library: Translations of the Writings of the Fathers Down to A.D. 325*, ed. Alexander Roberts and James Donaldson (Edinburgh: T.& T. Clark, 1869), 46–47.

59. Cf. Hubert Cancik, "Die frühesten antiken Texte zu den Begriffen 'Menschenrecht', 'Religionsfreiheit', 'Toleranz'" [The earliest ancient texts on the terms "human right," "freedom of religion," "tolerance"], in *Menschenrechte und europäische Identität—die antiken Grundlagen* [Human rights and European identity: The ancient foundations], ed. Klaus M. Girardet, Ulrich Nortmann (Stuttgart: Franz Steiner, 2005), 98–100.

60. Cf. Henri-Xavier Arquillière, *L'augustinisme politique: Essai sur la formation des théories politiques du Moyen-Âge* [Political Augustinism: Essay on the development of medieval political theory] (Paris: Vrin, 1955).

61. Cf. Gregory the Great, "Epistola LXV," in *Patrologia Latina 77* (Paris: Imprimerie Catholique, 1844 ff.), 663B.

62. Martin Rhonheimer, *Christentum und säkularer Staat. Geschichte—Gegenwart—Zukunft* [Christianity and the secular state: Past—present—future] (Freiburg i. B.: Herder, 2014), 71–72. Translated from the German.

63. Dreier, *Staat ohne Gott* [State without God], 9. Translated from the German.

64. Pope Pius VI, *Quod Aliquantum*, https://www.vatican.va/content/pius-vi/it/documents/breve-quod-aliquantum-10-marzo-1791.html. Translated from the Italian.

65. Pope Gregory XVI, *Mirari Vos Arbitramur*, https://www.vatican.va/content/gregorius-xvi/it/documents/encyclica-mirari-vos-15-augusti-1832.html. Translated from the Italian.

66. Pope Pius IX, *Quanta Cura*, https://www.vatican.va/content/pius-ix/la/documents/encyclica-quanta-cura-8-decembris-1864.html. Translated from the Latin.

67. Cf. Rhonheimer, *Christentum und säkularer Staat* [Christianity and the secular state], 149–55.

68. Cf. Alfredo Ottaviani, *Institutiones iuris publici ecclesiastici*, vol. 2 (Rome: Typis polyglottis Vaticanis, 1960), 72–73.

69. Even Pope Pius XII, in a supposedly tolerant address of 1953, maintains that "truth is fundamentally more valuable than freedom, and that therefore the state must not give falsehood a right to existence, dissemination, or action," as quoted in Jan-Heiner Tück, "Von der Zitadelle zur offenen Stadt: Geschichtliche Selbstvergewisserung und dialogische Öffnung auf dem Zweiten Vatikanum" [From citadel to open city: Historical self-assurance and dialogical opening in the Second Vatican Council], in *Zukunft aus der Geschichte Gottes: Theologie im Dienst an einer Kirche für morgen: Für Peter Hünermann* [Future from the past of God: Theology in the service of a Church of tomorrow; For Peter Hünermann], ed. Guido Bausenhart, Margit Eckholt, and Linus Hauser (Freiburg i. B.: Herder, 2014), 166. Translated from the German.

70. For a grounding on the genesis of the text of the declaration on religious freedom, cf. Karl Gabriel, Christian Spieß, and Katja Winkler, *Wie fand der Katholizismus zur Religionsfreiheit? Faktoren der Erneuerung der katholischen Kirche* [How did Catholicism get to religious freedom? Factors of renewal in the Catholic Church] (Paderborn: Schöningh, 2016), 12–62.

71. Pope Paul VI, *Dignitatis Humanae* 2, https://www.vatican.va/archive/hist_councils/ii_vatican_council/documents/vat-ii_decl_19651207_dignitatis-humanae_en.html.

72. Cf. Marianne Heimbach-Steins, *Religionsfreiheit: Ein Menschenrecht unter Druck* [Religious freedom: A human right under pressure] (Paderborn: Schöningh, 2012), 79–80.

73. Pope Paul VI, *Dignitatis Humanae* 2.

74. Pope Paul VI, *Dignitatis Humanae* 6.

75. Pope Paul VI, *Dignitatis Humanae* 6.

76. Pope Paul VI, *Dignitatis Humanae* 13.

77. Ernst-Wolfgang Böckenförde, "Die Religionsfreiheit im Spannungsfeld zwischen Kirche und Staat" [Religious freedom in tension between Church and state], in Ernst-Wolfgang Böckenförde, *Religionsfreiheit: Die Kirche in der modernen Welt* [Religious freedom: The Church in the modern world] (Freiburg i. B.: Herder, 1990), 46.

78. Cf. Otto Hermann Pesch, *Das Zweite Vatikanische Konzil. Vorgeschichte—Verlauf—Ergebnisse—Wirkungsgeschichte* [The Second Vatican Council: Prehistory—course—results—influence] (Kevelaer: Topos, 2012), 169.

79. Pope Paul VI, *Dignitatis Humanae* 1.

80. Pope Paul VI, *Dignitatis Humanae* 15.

81. Pope Paul VI, *Dignitatis Humanae* 9.

82. As Hans Joas suggests, the idea of human rights can indeed be seen as a "further development of Judeo-Christian motifs"—but it must always be remembered that this development was propagated outside the Catholic Church and managed to win through only despite bitter opposition from the Church. Hans Joas, *Die Sakralität der Person: Eine neue Genealogie der Menschenrechte* [The sacral nature of the person: A new genealogy of human rights] (Berlin: Suhrkamp, 2011), 106. Translated from the German.

83. The Western Church's practice of killing heretics is based on political Augustinism, which viewed the state as the worldly arm of the Church, so that it was empowered or even obligated to kill those which the Church handed over as heretics. At the same time, it must be emphasized that this constellation represents not only an ecclesiastical use of the state, but also temporal rulers' wishes to consolidate their power through self-sacralization—not that this point does credit to either side. Cf. Arnold Angenendt, *Toleranz und Gewalt: Das Christentum zwischen Bibel und Schwert* [Tolerance and violence: Christianity between Bible and sword] (Münster: Aschendorff, 2018), 245–62.

84. Pope Benedict XVI, "The Listening Heart: Reflections on the Foundations of Law; Address of His Holiness Benedict XVI," https://www.vatican.va/content/benedict-xvi/en/speeches/2011/september/documents/hf_ben-xvi_spe_20110922_reichstag-berlin.html.

85. Pope Benedict XVI, "The Listening Heart."

4. CONCEPTIONS OF REFORM

1. Cf. Eike Wolgast, "Reform/Reformation" [Reform/reformation], in *Geschichtliche Grundbegriffe: Historisches Lexikon zur politisch-sozialen Sprache in Deutschland* [Basic historical terms: A historical lexicon of sociopolitical speech in Germany], ed. Otto Brunner, Werner Conze, and Reinhart Koselleck, vol. 5 (Stuttgart: Klett-Cotta, 2004), 313–60; Anselm Schubert, "Wie die Reformation zu ihrem Namen kam" [How the Reformation got its name] *Archiv für Reformationsgeschichte* 107 (2016): 343–54; and Wietse de Boer, "Reformation(s) and counter-reformation(s)," in *Martin Luther: A Christian between Reform and Modernity*, ed. Alberto Melloni, vol. 1 (Berlin: De Gruyter 2017), 43–58.

2. Andreas Gasser, *Form und Materie bei Aristoteles: Vorarbeiten zu einer Interpretation der Substanzbücher* [Form and matter in Aristotle: Preliminary studies on an interpretation of the *Metaphysics*, Books Zeta, Eta, and Thau] (Tübingen: Mohr Siebeck, 2015), 91.

3. Niklas Luhmann, *Funktion der Religion* [The function of religion] (Frankfurt a. M.: Suhrkamp, 1982), 26. Translated from the German. For a theologically contextualized interpretation, see Michael Seewald, "Religion als Kontingenzbewältigung? Präzisierungen zu einem gängigen Topos in Auseinandersetzung mit Niklas Luhmann, Hermann Lübbe und Ernst Tugendhat" [Religion as coping with contingency? Concretizing a common trope through engagement with Niklas Luhmann, Hermann Lübbe, and Ernst Tugendhat] *Jahrbuch für Religionsphilosophie* 15 (2016): 155–70.

4. Luhmann, *Funktion der Religion*, 21–22. Translated from the German.

5. Pope Paul VI. *Gaudium et Spes* 1, https://www.vatican.va/archive/hist_councils/ii_vatican_council/documents/vat-ii_cons_19651207_gaudium-et-spes_en.html.

6. See Gerhard Müller, ed., *Theologische Realenzyklopeädie* [Theological encyclopedia], vol. 28, s.v. "Reformation" (Berlin: De Gruyter, 1997), 389.

7. Johannes Spörl, "Das Alte und das Neue im Mittelalter: Studien zum Problem des mittelalterlichen Fortschrittsbewußt-

seins" [The old and the new in the Middle Ages: Studies on the problem of a medieval awareness of progress], *Historisches Jahrbuch* 50 (1930): 309. Translated from the German.

8. See e.g., Karl Shuve, "Cyprian of Carthage's writings from the rebaptism controversy: Two revisionary proposals reconsidered," *Journal of Theological Studies* 61, no. 2 (2010): 634n27.

9. Kurt Bayertz, "Was könnte mit der These gemeint sein, dass der Mensch die Geschichte macht?" [What might the thesis mean that people make history?], in *Die Gestaltbarkeit der Geschichte* [The ability to shape history], ed. Kurt Bayertz and Matthias Hoesch (Hamburg: Felix Meiner, 2019), 33. Translated from the German.

10. Barbara Stollberg-Rilinger, "Was heißt Ideengeschichte?" [What does "history of ideas" mean?], in *Ideengeschichte* [History of ideas], ed. Barbara Stollberg-Rilinger (Stuttgart: Franz Steiner, 2010), 42. Translated from the German.

11. Joseph Ratzinger, "Bemerkungen zum Schema 'De fontibus revelationis'" [Remarks on the schema "De fontibus revelationis"], in Joseph Ratzinger, *Gesammelte Schriften 7/1: Zur Lehre des Zweiten Vatikanischen Konzils* [Collected writings 7/1: On the doctrine of the Second Vatican Council] (Freiburg i. B.: Herder, 2012), 162. Translated from the German.

12. Marcel Lefebvre, *Ich klage das Konzil an!* [I accuse the Council!] (Stuttgart: Sarto, 2009), 117–18. Translated from the German.

13. Pope Paul VI, *Lumen Gentium* 8, https://www.vatican.va/archive/hist_councils/ii_vatican_council/documents/vat-ii_const_19641121_lumen-gentium_en.html. Cf. also Peter Neuner, "Antimodernismus des 19. und 20. Jahrhunderts: Eine historische Perspektive" [The antimodernism of the 19th and 20th centuries: A historical perspective], in *"Nicht außerhalb derWelt": Theologie und Soziologie* ["Not outside the world: Theology and sociology], ed. Magnus Striet, (Freiburg i. B.: Herder, 2014), 86.

14. For more on this phenomenon, see Michael Seewald, "Sakramententheologie—mit einem oder mit zwei Augen? Eine (nicht nur) dogmatische Nachlese zum Kommunionstreit" [Sacramental theology—with one eye or two? A (not just)

dogmatic investigation into the debate over communion], in *Eucharistie—Kirche—Ökumene: Aspekte und Hintergründe des Kommunionstreits* [Eucharist—Church—ecumenism: Aspects and backgrounds on the debate over Communion], ed. Thomas Söding and Wolfgang Thönissen (Freiburg i. B.: Herder, 2019), 172–88.

15. Pope Benedict XVI, "Christmas Greetings to the Members of the Roman Curia and the Prelature," December 22, 2005, https://www.vatican.va/content/benedict-xvi/en/speeches/ 2005/december/documents/hf_ben_xvi_spe_20051222 _roman-curia.html.

16. Benedict XVI, "Christmas Greetings."

17. Benedict XVI, "Christmas Greetings."

18. Aaron Langenfeld, "Kirche als Subjekt der Einheit? Anmerkungen zu Thomas Marschlers Begriff von Dogmengeschichte im Kontext der Frage nach einer Einheit der Theologien" [Church as subject of unity? Remarks on Thomas Marschler's conception of dogmatic history in the context of the question of theological unity], in *Stile der Theologie: Einheit und Vielfalt katholischer Systematik in der Gegenwart* [Styles of theology: Unity and plurality of Catholic systematics in the present], ed. Martin Dürnberger, Aaron Langenfeld, Magnus Lerch and Melanie Wurst (Regensburg: Friedrich Pustet, 2017), 174.

19. A more thorough presentation of the approach of Hugh of St. Victor may be found in Michael Seewald, *Dogma im Wandel: Wie Glaubenslehren sich entwickeln* [Dogmas undergoing transformation: How doctrines of faith develop] (Freiburg i. B.: Herder, 2018), 156–67.

20. Hugh of St. Victor, *Hugh of Saint Victor on the Sacraments of the Christian Faith (De Sacramentis)*, trans. Roy J. Deferrari (Eugene, OR: Wipf & Stock Publishers, 2007), 169.

21. Hugh of St. Victor, *On the Sacraments*, 177. Emphasis added.

22. Stefan Schreiber, "Von der Verkündigung Jesu zum verkündigten Christus" [From Jesus's proclamation to the proclaimed Christ], in *Christologie* [Christology], ed. Karlheinz Ruhstorfer (Paderborn: utb, 2018), 82–83. Translated from the German.

23. Andreas Lindemann, "'Wir glauben an Jesus Christus...': Glaube und Bekenntnis im frühen Christentum zwischen Integration und Abgrenzung" ["We believe in Jesus Christ...": Faith and confession in early Christianity between integration and distinction], in *Die Rede von Jesus Christus als Glaubensaussage: Der zweite Artikel des Apostolischen Glaubensbekenntnisses im Gespräch zwischen Bibelwissenschaft und Dogmatik* [Speaking of Jesus Christ as a statement of faith: The second article of the Apostles' Creed in the dialogue between Bible scholarship and dogmatics], ed. Jens Herzer, Anne Käfer, and Jörg Frey (Tübingen: Utb, 2018), 28. Translated from the German.

24. Cf. Helmut Merklein, "Zum Verständnis des paulinischen Begriffs 'Evangelium'" [On understanding the Pauline term "gospel"], in Helmut Merklein, *Studien zu Jesus und Paulus I* [Studies on Jesus and Paul I] (Tübingen: Mohr Siebeck, 1987), 279–95; and Ferdinand Hahn, *Theologie des Neuen Testaments: Band 1: Die Vielfalt des Neuen Testaments* [The theology of the New Testament, vol. 1: The plurality of the New Testament], 2nd rev. ed. (Tübingen: Mohr Siebeck 2005), 180–322.

25. Hahn, *Theologie des neuen Testaments* [The theology of the New Testament], 190. Translated from the German.

26. Kasper, "Dogma unter dem Wort Gottes" [Dogma under the word of God], 57. Translated from the German.

27. Jürgen Werbick, *Einführung in die theologische Wissenschaftslehre* [Introduction to the science of theology] (Freiburg i. B.: Herder 2010), 188. Emphasis added. Translated from the German.

28. Walter Kasper, "Dogma unter dem Wort Gottes" [Dogma under the word of God], 146–47. Translated from the German. A similarly critical listing of possible defects in dogma—"rash," "supercilious," "guilty," "full of temptation," "meddlesome," and indeed "sinful in speech"—can be found in Karl Rahner, "Was ist eine dogmatische Aussage?" [What is a dogmatic ruling?], in *Karl Rahner: Sämtliche Werke 12: Menschsein und Menschwerdung Gottes: Studien zur Grundlegung der Dogmatik, der Christologie, Theologischen Anthropologie und Eschatologie* [Complete works 12: God's being human and becoming human; Studies on the foundations of dogmatics, Christology, theological

anthropology, and eschatology] (Freiburg i. B.: Herder, 2005), 153. Translated from the German.

29. Bruno Schüller, *Die Begründung sittlicher Urteile: Typen ethischer Argumentation in der Moraltheologie* [The justification of moral judgments: Types of ethical argumentation in moral theology] (Düsseldorf: Patmos, 1987), 313. Translated from the German.

30. Second Vatican Council, *Dei Verbum* 2, https://www.vatican.va/archive/hist_councils/ii_vatican_council/documents/vat-ii_const_19651118_dei-verbum_en.html.

31. Gunther Wenz, "Pannenbergs Kreis: Genese und erste Kritik eines theologischen Programms" [The Pannenberg circle: Development and initial assessment of a theological program], in *Offenbarung als Geschichte: Implikationen und Konsequenzen eines theologischen Programms* [Revelation as history: Implications and consequences of a theological program], ed. Gunter Wenz (Göttingen: Vandenhoeck & Ruprecht, 2018), 31. Translated from the German.

32. Second Vatican Council, *Lumen Gentium* 8.

33. Elmar Salmann, *Der geteilte Logos: Zum offenen Prozeß von neuzeitlichem Denken und Theologie* [The divided *logos*: On the open case of modern thought and theology] (Rome: Pontificio Ateneo S. Anselmo, 1992), 45–46. Translated from the German.

34. Bertram Stubenrauch, *Dialogisches Dogma: Der christliche Auftrag zur interreligiösen Begegnung* [Dialogical dogma: The Christian task of interreligious encounter] (Freiburg i. B.: Herder, 1995), 52.

35. Cf. Roman A. Siebenrock, "'Zeichen der Zeit': Zur Operationalisierung des christlichen Bekenntnisses vom universalen Heilswillen Gottes" ["Signs of the times": On the operationalization of the Christian profession for God's universal salvific will], *Zeitschrift für Katholische Theologie* 136 (2014): 48: "I consider this Christologically specified and pneumatologically dynamized reality of God's salvation at every possible present and all possible times to be the 'fundamental dogma' or the fundamental matrix of the Council." Translated from the German.

36. Cf. Second Vatican Council, *Lumen Gentium* 10.

37. Cf. Eugen Biser, "Der Spiegel des Glaubens: Zum Prozeß der theologischen Selbstkorrektur" [The mirror of faith: On the process of theological self-correction], in *Glaube als Lebensform: Der Beitrag Johann Baptist Hirschers zu Neugestaltung christlich-kirchlicher Lebenspraxis und lebensbezogener Theologie* [Faith as a way of life: Johann Baptist Hirscher's contribution to reshaping Christian ecclesiastical practices of life and life-centered theology], ed. Gebhard Fürst (Mainz: Matthias Grünewald, 1989), 139.

38. John Henry Newman, *An Essay on the Development of Christian Doctrine*, part 1, section 1, 7, https://www.newmanreader.org/works/development/index.html.

39. Peter Hünermann, *Dogmatische Prinzipienlehre: Glaube—Überlieferung—Theologie als Sprach und Wahrheitsgeschehen* [Dogmatic principles: Faith—tradition—theology as the occurrence of speech and truth] (Münster: Aschendorff, 2003), 259. Translated from the German.

40. Cf. Klaus Schatz, *Vaticanum I: 1869–1870. Band 3: Unfehlbarkeitsdiskussion und Rezeption* [Vatican I: 1869–1870, vol. 3: The discussion on infallibility and reception] (Paderborn: Schöningh, 1994), 140–47, and Pottmeyer, *Die Rolle des Papsttums* [The role of the papacy], 81–90.

41. Vincent Gasser, "Relatio" [Report] (July 11, 1870), in *Sacrorum Conciliorum Nova et Amplissima Collectio 52: Sacrosancti Oecumenici Concilii Vaticani (Pars 2)* [New and fullest collection of sacred councils 52: Holy ecumenical Vatican Council (part 2)] (Arnhem: H. Werner, 1877), 1214 A.

42. Second Vatican Council, *Lumen Gentium* 12.

43. A similar, though with respect to the existence of the Church more pragmatic, perspective may be found in Hans-Joachim Höhn, "Unfehlbar? Über die Suche nach existenziell verlässlichen Wahrheiten" [Infallible? On the search for existentially reliable truths], in *Glaube ohne Wahrheit? Theologie und Kirche vor den Anfragen des Relativismus* [Faith without truth? Theology and Church in the face of relativism's questioning], ed. Michael Seewald (Freiburg i. B.: Herder, 2018), 134–35: "If a particular statement of the Church magisterium cannot be proved to be a way of encountering the Christian message to which one can do justice only by trusting in its existential

truth, then the statement can no longer be considered a performative statement (of faith) whose truth can be determined only by following it. In such a case, teachings uttered with a claim to bindingness can no longer demand reception....For example, if it should be attempted to continue justifying the canon law rule against ordination of women on purely historical grounds (or additionally through absurd claims about the theological relevance of sex differences) and to use these arguments to elevate the rule to the level of dogma, then the corresponding claim to validity would be impossible to back up." Translated from the German.

44. Cf. Aristotle, *Nicomachean Ethics* VI 4–10 (1140a–1142b), trans. W. D. Ross, http://classics.mit.edu/Aristotle/nicomachaen .6.vi.html.

45. For the following, cf. Michael Seewald, "Worüber wird gestritten, wenn Glaubenslehren sich entwickeln? Ein kontingenztheoretischer Vorschlag" [What is being debated when doctrines develop? A proposal from the point of view of contingency theory], *Münchener Theologische Zeitschrift* 69 (2018): 284–86.

46. Hartmut A. G. Bosinsksi, "Eine Normvariante menschlicher Beziehungsfähigkeit: Homosexualität aus Sicht der Sexualmedizin" [A normal variant of the human capacity for relationship: Homosexuality in the eyes of sexual medicine], in *"Wer bin ich, ihn zu verurteilen?" Homosexualität und katholische Kirche* ["Who am I to judge?" Homosexuality and the Catholic Church], ed. Stephan Goertz (Freiburg i. B.: Herder, 2015), 91–130.

47. Second Vatican Council, *Gaudium et Spes* 48.

48. *Catechism of the Catholic Church* 2357.

49. *Catechism of the Catholic Church* 2359.

50. *Code of Canon Law*, canon 1055, §1.

51. Rahel Jaeggi, *Kritik von Lebensformen* [Criticizing ways of life] (Frankfurt a. M.: Suhrkamp, 2014), 261. Translated from the German.

52. Second Vatican Council, *Gaudium et Spes* 5.

53. Klaus Mertes, "Totschlagargument Zeitgeist" [Zeitgeist as a discussion ender], *Stimmen der Zeit* 236 (2018): 226. Translated from the German.

5. OUTLOOK

1. Johann Michael Sailer, *Vernunftlehre für Menschen wie sie sind, d.i. Anleitung zur Erkenntniß und Liebe der Wahrheit III. Band* [Theory of reason for people as they are, i.e., instruction on insight and love of the truth, vol. 3], 2nd ed. rev. (Munich: Johann Baptist Strobel, 1795), 332, https://www.digitale-sammlungen.de/en/view/bsb10044283. Translated from the German.

2. Cf. Klaus Unterburger, "'Reform der ganzen Kirche': Konturen, Ursachen und Wirkungen einer Leitidee und Zwangsvorstellung im Spätmittelalter" ["Reform of the entire Church": Outlines, causes, and effects of a late medieval guiding idea and obsession], in *Reformen in der Kirche: Historische Perspektiven* [Reforms in the Church: Historical perspectives], ed. Andreas Merkt, Günther Wassilowsky and Gregor Wurst (Freiburg i. B.: Herder, 2014), 116f.

3. Sailer, *Vernunftlehre* [Theory of reason], 335. Translated from the German.

BIBLIOGRAPHY

Catechism of the Catholic Church, https://www.vatican.va/
archive/ENG0015/_INDEX.HTM.

Codex Iuris Canonici/Code of Canon Law, https://www.vatican
.va/archive/cod-iuris-canonici/cic_index_en.html.

Various bulls, encyclicals, and other papal writings both in
Latin and in translation were likewise accessed through the web-
site of the Holy See (www.vatican.va), where they are available
under the subsite of the authoring pontiff.

*Acta Synodalia Sacrosancti Concilii Oecumenici Vaticani II
(Volumen 1, pars 4: Congregationes generales XXXI–
XXXVI)* [Synodal Acts of the Holy Ecumenical Second
Vatican Council (volume 1, part 4: General congregations
31–36)]. Vatican City: Typis Polyglottis Vaticanis, 1971.

Aner, Karl. "Die *Historia dogmatum* des Abtes Jerusalem" [The
historia dogmatum of Abbot Jerusalem]. *Zeitschrift für
Kirchengeschichte* 10 (1928): 76–103.

Angenendt, Arnold. *Geschichte der Religiösität im Mittelalter*
[History of religiousness in the Middle Ages]. Darmstadt:
Wissenschaftliche Buchgesellschaft, 2009.

————. *Toleranz und Gewalt: Das Christentum zwischen Bibel
und Schwert* [Tolerance and violence: Christianity between
Bible and sword]. Münster: Aschendorff, 2018.

Aristotle. *Nicomachean Ethics*. Translated by W. D. Ross. http://
classics.mit.edu/Aristotle/nicomachaen.html.

————. *Topics: Part I*. Translated by W. A. Pickard-Cambridge.
http://classics.mit.edu/Aristotle/topics.html.

Arkes, Hardley, et al. "An Appeal to the Cardinals of the Catholic Church." https://www.firstthings.com/web-exclusives/2018/08/an-appeal-to-the-cardinals-of-the-catholic-church.

Arquillière, Henri-Xavier. *L'augustinisme politique: Essai sur la formation des théories politiques du Moyen-Âge* [Political Augustinism: Essay on the development of medieval political theory]. Paris: Vrin, 1955.

Augustine. *De trinitate libri XV* [The fifteen books of *On the Trinity*]. Edited by W. J. Mountain and F. Glorie. Turnhout: Brepols, 1968.

———. *De vera religione*. In *De doctrina christiana; De vera religione* [On Christian doctrine; On true religion]. Edited by K. D. Daur and J. Martin. Turnhout: Brepols, 1962.

Bayertz, Kurt. "Was könnte mit der These gemeint sein, dass der Mensch die Geschichte macht?" [What might the thesis mean that people make history?]. In *Die Gestaltbarkeit der Geschichte* [The ability to shape history], edited by Kurt Bayertz and Matthias Hoesch, 19–38. Hamburg: Felix Meiner, 2019.

Beck, Ulrich. *Der eigene Gott: Friedensfähigkeit und Gewaltpotential der Religionen* [One's own God: Religions' capacity for peace and potential for violence]. Frankfurt a. M.: Insel Verlag, 2008.

Beinert, Wolfgang, and Bertram Stubenrauch, eds.. *Neues Lexikon der Dogmatik* [New dictionary of dogmatics]. Freiburg i. B.: Herder, 2012.

Berger, Peter L. *Der Zwang zur Häresie: Religion in der pluralistischen Gesellschaft* [Compelled to heresy: Religion in pluralist society]. Freiburg i. B.: Herder, 1992.

Bier, Georg. "Frauen weihen?" [Ordaining women?]. *Herder Korrespondenz* 71, no. 8 (2017): 45–47.

Biser, Eugen. "Der Spiegel des Glaubens: Zum Prozeß der theologischen Selbstkorrektur" [The mirror of faith: On the process of theological self-correction]. In *Glaube als Lebensform: Der Beitrag Johann Baptist Hirschers zu Neugestaltung christlich-kirchlicher Lebenspraxis und lebensbezogener Theologie* [Faith as a way of life: Johann Baptist Hirscher's contribution to the reshaping of Christian ecclesiastical practices of life and life-centered theology], edited by Gebhard Fürst. Mainz: Matthias Grünewald, 1989, 139–149.

Blumenberg, Hans. *Die Legitimität der Neuzeit* [The legitimacy of modernity]. Rev. ed. Frankfurt a. M.: Suhrkamp, 2016.

Böckenförde, Ernst-Wolfgang. "Die Religionsfreiheit im Spannungsfeld zwischen Kirche und Staat" [Religious freedom in tension between Church and state]. In *Religionsfreiheit: Die Kirche in der modernen Welt* [Religious freedom: The Church in the modern world], edited by Ernst-Wolfgang Böckenförde, 33–58. Freiburg i. B.: Herder, 1990.

Boer, Wietse de. "Reformation(s) and counter-reformation(s)." In *Martin Luther: A Christian between Reform and Modernity*, edited by Alberto Melloni, 1:43–58. Berlin: De Gruyter, 2017.

Bosinski, Hartmut A. G. "Eine Normvariante menschlicher Beziehungsfähigkeit: Homosexualität aus Sicht der Sexualmedizin" [A normal variant of the human capacity for relationship: Homosexuality in the eyes of sexual medicine]. In *"Wer bin ich, ihn zu verurteilen?" Homosexualität und katholische Kirche* ["Who am I to judge?" Homosexuality and the Catholic Church], edited by Stephan Goertz, 91–130. Freiburg i. B.: Herder, 2015.

Boulanger, Mr. [pseudonym of Paul Thiry d'Holbach]. *Le christianisme dévoilé ou examen des principes et des effets de la religion chrétienne* [Christianity unveiled, or: An Examination of the principles and effects of the Christian religion]. London [actually Nancy, France]: [no publisher named], 1767.

Brinkmann, Bernhard. "Die Apostolische Konstitution Pius XII. 'Sacramentum Ordinis' vom 30. November 1947" [Pius XII's Apostolic Constitution 'Sacramentum Ordinis' of November 30, 1947]. *Theologische Quartalsschrift* 130 (1950): 311–36.

———. "Enthält die Apostolische Konstitution 'Sacramentum Ordinis' Pius' XII. eine Kathedralentscheidung?" [Does Pius XII's Apostolic Constitution 'Sacramentum Ordinis' contain an ex cathedra ruling?]. *Theologische Quartalsschrift* 136 (1956): 314–24.

Burkard, Dominik. "Schwierigkeiten bei der Beschäftigung mit der päpstlichen Zensur im ausgehenden 18. Jahrhundert:

Am Beispiel der 'Causa Isenbiehl'" [Difficulties in examining papal censorship in the late 18th century: Using the example of the 'Isenbiehl case']. In *Verbotene Bücher. Zur Geschichte des Index im 18. und 19. Jahrhundert* [Banned books: On the history of the Index in the 18th and 19th centuries], edited by Hubert Wolf, 299–316. Paderborn: Schöningh, 2008.

Cancik, Hubert. "Die frühesten antiken Texte zu den Begriffen 'Menschenrecht,' 'Religionsfreiheit,' 'Toleranz'" [The earliest ancient texts on the terms "human right," "freedom of religion," "tolerance"]. In *Menschenrechte und europäische Identität—die antiken Grundlagen* [Human rights and European identity: The ancient foundations], edited by Klaus M. Girardet, Ulrich Nortmann, 94–104. Stuttgart: Franz Steiner, 2005.

Clement of Rome. *See under* Quasten, Johannes.

d'Alembert, Jean le Rond. *Essai sur les éléments de philosophie* [Essay on the elements of philosophy], edited by Richard N. Schwab, 1805; repr., Hildesheim: Olm, 2003.

Dassmann, Ernst. *Ämter und Dienste in den frühchristlichen Gemeinden* [Offices and services in the early Christian congregations]. Bonn: Borengässer, 1994.

Davis, Kathleen. *Periodization and Sovereignty: How Ideas of Feudalism and Secularization Govern the Politics of Time.* Philadelphia: University of Pennsylvania, 2008.

de la Torre, Joaquín Salaverri. "El valor de las Enciclicas a la luz de la 'Humani generis'" [The significance of the encyclicals in light of *Humani generis*]. *Miscelanea Comillas* 17 (1952): 135–71.

Diderot, Denis et al., eds. *Encyclopédie ou dictionnaire raisonné des sciences, des arts et des métiers.* Paris/Neuchâtel, 1765ff. https://encyclopedie.uchicago.edu.

Dietrich, Stephan, ed. *Gotthart Wunberg: Jahrhundertwende; Studien zur Literatur der Moderne; Zum 70. Geburtstag des Autors* [Gotthart Wunberg: Turn of the century; Studies on the literature of modernity; for the author's seventieth birthday]. Tübingen: Narr, 2001.

Dreier, Horst. *Staat ohne Gott: Religion in der säkulären Moderne* [State without God: Religion in secular modernity]. Munich: C. H. Beck, 2018.

Ebeling, Gerhard. *Die Geschichtlichkeit der Kirche und ihrer Verkündigung als theologisches Problem* [The historicity of the Church and its preaching as a theological problem]. Tübingen: Mohr, 1954.

Eichmann, Eduard. *Lehrbuch des Kirchenrechts auf Grund des Codex Iuris Canonici* [Textbook of Church law, based on the *Code of Canon Law*]. Vol. 3. Revised by Klaus Mörsdorf. Paderborn: Schöningh, 1950.

Eisenstadt, Shmuel. *Comparative Civilizations and Multiple Modernities*. Vol. 1. Boston: Brill, 2003.

Flüchter, Antje. "Der transkulturelle Vergleich zwischen Komparatistik und Transkulturalität" [Transcultural comparisons between comparative studies and transculturality]. In *Monarchische Herrschaftsformen der Vormoderne in transkultureller Perspektive* [Transcultural perspectives on monarchic forms of sovereignty in the pre-modern era], edited by Wolfram Drews, Antje Flüchter, et al., 1–32. Berlin: De Gruyter, 2015.

Frey, Christofer. *Mysterium der Kirche—Öffnung zur Welt: Zwei Aspekte der Erneuerung französischer katholischer Theologie* [Mystery of the Church—opening toward the world: Two aspects in the renewal of French Catholic theology]. Göttingen: Vandenhoeck & Ruprecht, 1969.

Fürst, Alfons. "Die Entstehung der kirchlichen Ämter und Strukturen" [The development of Church offices and structures]. In Franz Xaver Bischof, Thomas Bremer, Giancarlo Collet, and Alfons Fürst. *Einführung in die Geschichte des Christentums* [Introduction to the history of Christianity]. Freiburg i. B.: Herder, 2012.

Fustel de Coulanges, Numa Denis. *La cité antique. Étude sur le culte, le droit, les institutions de la Grèce et de Rome* [The ancient city: Study on the religion, law, and institutions of Greece and Rome]. Paris: Durand, 1864.

Gabriel, Karl, Christian Spieß, and Katja Winkler. *Wie fand der Katholizismus zur Religionsfreiheit? Faktoren der Erneuerung der katholischen Kirche* [How did Catholicism get to religious freedom? Factors of renewal in the Catholic Church]. Paderborn: Schöningh, 2016.

Gasser, Andreas. *Form und Materie bei Aristoteles: Vorarbeiten zu einer Interpretation der Substanzbücher* [Form and matter in Aristotle: Preliminary studies on an interpretation of the *Metaphysics*, books Zeta, Eta, and Thau]. Tübingen: Mohr Siebeck, 2015.

Gasser, Vincent. "Relatio" [Report] (July 11, 1870). In *Sacrorum Conciliorum Nova et Amplissima Collectio 52: Sacrosancti Oecumenici Concilii Vaticani (Pars 2)* [New and fullest collection of sacred councils 52: Holy ecumenical Vatican Council (Part 2)]. Arnhem: H. Werner, 1877.

Graeber, Andreas. Auctoritas patrum*: Formen und Wege der Senatsherrschaft zwischen Politik und Tradition* [*Auctoritas patrum*: Forms and pathways of senate rule between politics and tradition]. Berlin: Springer, 2001.

Graf, Friedrich Wilhelm. *Missbrauchte Götter: Zum Menschenbilderstreit in der Moderne* [Misused gods: On the dispute over the human image in modernity]. Munich: C. H. Beck, 2009.

Guthrie King, Colin. "Sokratische Ignoranz und aristotelische Anerkennung: Über den Umgang mit Autorität und Zeugnissen in der antiken Philosophie" [Socratic ignorance and Aristotelian recognition: On dealing with authority and testimony in ancient philosophy]. In *Transformationen antiker Wissenschaften* [Transformations of ancient sciences], edited by Georg Toepfer and Hartmut Böhme, 35–62. Berlin: De Gruyter, 2010.

Gutmann, Thomas. "Religion und normative Moderne" [Religion and normative modernity]. In *Moderne und Religion: Kontroversen um Modernität und Säkularisierung* [Modernity and religion: Controversies surrounding modernity and secularlization], edited by Ulrich Willems et al., 447–88. Bielefeld: transcript, 2013.

Habermas, Jürgen. "Modernity—an Incomplete Project." Translated by Seyla Ben-Habib. In *The Anti-aesthetic: Essays on Postmodern Culture*, edited by Hal Foster, 3–15. Port Townsend, WA: Bay Press, 1983.

————. "Modernity's Consciousness of Time and Its Need for Self-Reassurance." In Jürgen Habermas, *The Philosophical Discourse of Modernity: Twelve Lectures*, 1–22. Translated by Frederick Lawrence. Maldon, MA: Polity, 1990.

Hahn, Ferdinand. *Theologie des Neuen Testaments: Band 1: Die Vielfalt des Neuen Testaments* [The theology of the New Testament. Vol. 1: The plurality of the New Testament]. 2nd rev. ed. Tübingen: Mohr Siebeck 2005.

Harmer, Thomas. *Beobachtungen über den Orient aus Reisebeschreibungen, zur Aufklärung der heiligen Schrift* [Observations on the Orient from travelogues, for the purpose of enlightenment of the Holy Scriptures]. Vol. 1. Translated and with commentary by Johann Ernst Faber. Hamburg: Johannes Carl Bohn, 1772. https://www.digitale-sammlungen.de/en/view/bsb11428969.

Heimbach-Steins, Marianne. *Religionsfreiheit: Ein Menschenrecht unter Druck* [Religious freedom: A human right under pressure]. Paderborn: Schöningh, 2012.

Hirscher, Johann Baptist. *Die christliche Moral als Lehre von der Verwirklichung des göttlichen Reiches in der Menschheit* [Christian morality as the teaching of realizing the divine kingdom in humanity]. Vol. 3. Tübingen: Thiessing, 1836.

Hoffmann-Rehnitz, Philip, André Krischer, and Matthias Pohlig. "Entscheiden als Problem der Geschichtswissenschaft" [Decision-making as a problem for the study of history]. *Zeitschrift für Historische Forschung* 45 (2018): 217–81.

Höhn, Hans-Joachim. "Unfehlbar? Über die Suche nach existenziell verlässlichen Wahrheiten" [Infallible? On the search for existentially reliable truths]. In *Glaube ohne Wahrheit? Theologie und Kirche vor den Anfragen des Relativismus* [Faith without truth? Theology and Church in the face of relativism's questioning], edited by Michael Seewald, 119–37. Freiburg i. B.: Herder, 2018.

Hugh of St. Victor. *Hugh of Saint Victor on the Sacraments of the Christian Faith (De Sacramentis)*. Translated by Roy J. Deferrari. Eugene, OR: Wipf & Stock Publishers, 2007.

Hünermann, Peter. *Dogmatische Prinzipienlehre: Glaube—Überlieferung—Theologie als Sprach und Wahrheitsgeschehen* [Dogmatic principles: Faith—Tradition—Theology as the occurrence of speech and truth]. Münster: Aschendorff, 2003.

———. "Die Herausbildung der Lehre von den definitiv zu haltenden Wahrheiten seit dem zweiten Vatikanischen Konzil" [The development since the Second Vatican Council of teaching on truths to be held definitively]. *Cristianesimo nella storia* 21 (2000): 71–101.

Hürth, Franz. "Constitutio Apostolica de Sacris Ordinibus Diaconatus, Presbyteratus, Episcopatus: Textus et Commentarius cum Appendice" [Apostolic Consistution on the holy ordination of deacons, presbyters, and bishops: Text and commentary including appendices]. *Periodica de re morali, canonica, liturgica* 37 (1948): 9–41.

Ignatius of Antioch. *See under* Quasten, Johannes.

Isenbiehl, Johann Lorenz. *Neuer Versuch über die Weissagung vom Emmanuel* [New essay on the prophecy of Emmanuel]. No place or publisher, 1778. Accessed at: https://www .digitale-sammlungen.de/en/view/bsb10411305.

Jaeggi, Rahel. *Kritik von Lebensformen* [Criticizing ways of life]. Frankfurt a. M.: Suhrkamp, 2014.

Jerusalem, Johann Friedrich Wilhelm. *Betrachtungen über die vornehmsten Wahrheiten der Religion* [Observations on the most preeminent truths of religion]. Vol. 1. Braunschweig: Fürstl. Waisenhaus-Buchandlung, 1785. Accessed at: https://collections.thulb.uni-jena.de/receive/HisBest _cbu_00032740?derivate=HisBest_derivate_00018948.

Joas, Hans. *Die Sakralität der Person: Eine neue Genealogie der Menschenrechte* [The sacral nature of the person: A new genealogy of human rights]. Berlin: Suhrkamp, 2011.

———. "Die säkulare Option: Ihr Aufstieg und ihre Folgen." [The secular option: Its rise and consequences]. In *Kommunitarismus und Religion* [Communitarianism and religion], edited by Michael Kühnlein, *Deutsche Zeitschrift für Philosophie*, special edition no. 25 (2010): 231–41.

Kant, Immanuel. "Beantwortung der Frage: Was ist Aufklärung?" [Answer to the question: What is enlightenment?]. *UTOPIE kreativ* 159 (2004): 5–10. (Reprint of 1784 original).

————. *Critique of Pure Reason.* Translated by Norman Kemp Smith. London: Macmillan, 1929. https://archive.org/details/in.ernet.dli.2015.222508.

Kany, Roland. *Augustins Trinitätsdenken: Bilanz, Kritik und Weiterführung der modernen Forschung zu De trinitate* [Augustin's notions of the trinity: Summary, criticism, and extension of modern scholarship on *De trinitate*]. Tübingen: Mohr Siebeck, 2007.

Kasper, Walter. "Dogma unter dem Wort Gottes" [Dogma under the word of God]. In Walter Kasper, *Gesammelte Schriften 7: Evangelien und Dogma. Grundlegung der Dogmatik* [Collected writings 7: Gospels and dogma. Foundations of dogmatics], 43–150. Freiburg i. B.: Herder, 2015.

Kaufmann, Franz Xaver. *Kirche in der ambivalenten Moderne* [The Church in ambivalent modernity]. Freiburg i. B.: Herder, 2012.

Kleutgen, Joseph. *Die Theologie der Vorzeit* [The theology of prehistory]. Vol. 1. Münster: Theissing, 1867, first ed. 1853.

Langenfeld, Aaron. "Kirche als Subjekt der Einheit? Anmerkungen zu Thomas Marschlers Begriff von Dogmengeschichte im Kontext der Frage nach einer Einheit der Theologien" [Church as subject of unity? Remarks on Thomas Marschler's conception of dogmatic history in the context of the question of theological unity]. In *Stile der Theologie: Einheit und Vielfalt katholischer Systematik in der Gegenwart* [Styles of theology: Unity and plurality of Catholic systematics in the present], edited by Martin Dürnberger, Aaron Langenfeld, Magnus Lerch, and Melanie Wurst, 169–79. Regensburg: Friedrich Pustet, 2017.

Lefebvre, Marcel. *Ich klage das Konzil an!* [I accuse the Council!]. Stuttgart: Sarto, 2009.

Leppin, Hartmut. *Die frühen Christen: Von den Anfängen bis Konstantin* [The early Christians: From the beginnings to Constantine]. Munich: C. H. Beck, 2018.

Lessing, Gotthold Ephraim. *Über den Beweis des Geistes und der Kraft* [On the proof of the Spirit and the Power]. Braunschweig: [no publisher given], 1777. Accessed at: https://www.digitale-sammlungen.de/en/view/bsb10927792.

Lindemann, Andreas. "'Wir glauben an Jesus Christus...': Glaube und Bekenntnis im frühen Christentum zwischen Integration und Abgrenzung" ["We believe in Jesus Christ...": Faith and confession in early Christianity between integration and distinction]. In *Die Rede von Jesus Christus als Glaubensaussage: Der zweite Artikel des Apostolischen Glaubensbekenntnisses im Gespräch zwischen Bibelwissenschaft und Dogmatik* [Speaking of Jesus Christ as a statement of faith: The second article of the Apostles' Creed in the dialogue between Bible scholarship and dogmatics], edited by Jens Herzer, Anne Käfer, and Jörg Frey, 19–53. Tübingen: Utb, 2018.

Lüdecke, Norbert. "Ein konsequenter Schritt. Kirchenrechtliche Überlegungen zu 'Professio fidei' und Treueeid" [A consistent step: Church law reflection on "Professo fidei" and vow of loyalty]. *Herder Korrespondenz* 54, no. 7 (2000): 339–44.

———. *Die Grundnormen des katholischen Lehrrechts in den päpstlichen Gesetzbüchern und neueren Äußerungen in päpstlicher Autorität* [The fundamental norms of Catholic magisterial law in papal law books and more recent statements in papal authority]. Würzburg: Echter, 1997.

Lüke, Ulrich. *"Als Anfang schuf Gott...": Bio-Theologie: Zeit—Evolution—Hominisation* ["As a beginning, God created...": Bio-theology: Time—evolution—hominization]. Paderborn: Schöningh, 1997.

Lubac, Henri de. *Die Kirche: Eine Betrachtung, übertragen und eingeleitet von Hans Urs von Balthasar* [The Church: A consideration, translated and with an introduction by Hans Urs von Balthasar]. Einsiedeln: Johannes, 2011.

Luhmann, Niklas. *Die Religion der Gesellschaft* [Society's religion], edited by André Kieserling. Frankfurt a. M.: Suhrkamp, 2000.

———. *Funktion der Religion* [The function of religion]. Frankfurt a. M.: Suhrkamp, 1982.

Martus, Steffen. *Aufklärung: Das deutsche 18. Jahrhundert: Ein Epochenbild* [Enlightenment: The German eighteenth century; Picture of an epoch]. Berlin: Rowohlt, 2015.

Merklein, Helmut. "Zum Verständnis des paulinischen Begriffs 'Evangelium'" [On understanding the Pauline term 'gospel']. In Helmut Merklein, *Studien zu Jesus und Paulus I* [Studies on Jesus and Paul I], 279–95. Tübingen: Mohr Siebeck, 1987.

Mertes, Klaus. "Totschlagargument Zeitgeist" [Zeitgeist as a discussion ender]. *Stimmen der Zeit* 236 (2018): 225–26.

Meuser, Bernhard. "Der verlorene Schlüssel: Warum Katechese den Katechismus braucht" [The lost key: Why catechesis requires the Catechism]. In *Kirche ohne Jugend: Ist die Glaubensweitergabe am Ende?* [Church without youth: Has the passing down of faith reached its end?], edited by Clauß Peter Sajak and Michael Langer, 109–19. Freiburg i. B.: Herder, 2018.

Möller, Horst. *Vernunft und Kritik: Deutsche Aufklärung im 17. und 18. Jahrhundert* [Reason and criticism: German Enlightenment in the 17th and 18th centuries]. Frankfurt a. M.: Suhrkamp, 1986.

Müller, Gerhard (ed.). *Theologische Realenzyklopeädie* [Theological encyclopedia]. Berlin: De Gruyter, 1997.

Neuner, Peter. "Antimodernismus des 19. und 20. Jahrhunderts: Eine historische Perspektive" [The anti-modernism of the 19th and 20th centuries: A historical perspective]. In *"Nicht außerhalb derWelt": Theologie und Soziologie* ["Not outside the world: Theology and sociology], edited by Magnus Striet, 61–92. Freiburg i. B.: Herder, 2014.

Newman, John Henry. *An Essay on the Development of Christian Doctrine*. https://www.newmanreader.org/works/development/index.html.

Oberthür, Franz. *Die Passivkorrespondenz Professor Franz Oberthürs* [The letters of Professor Franz Oberthür]. Vol. 1. Edited by Annemarie Lindig. Würzburg, privately printed, 1963.

Ottaviani, Alfredo. *Institutiones iuris publici ecclesiastici*. Vol. 2. Rome: Typis polyglottis Vaticanis, 1960.

Patrologia Graeca. Paris: Imprimerie Catholique, 1857 ff.

Patrologia Latina. Paris: Imprimerie Catholique, 1844 ff.

Pesch, Otto Hermann. *Das Zweite Vatikanische Konzil. Vorgeschichte—Verlauf—Ergebnisse—Wirkungsgeschichte*

[The Second Vatican Council: Prehistory—course—results—influence]. Kevelaer: Topos, 2012.

Pfister, Peter, ed. *Eugenio Pacelli—Pius XII (1876–1958) in the Assessment of Scholarship*. Regensburg: Schnell + Steiner, 2009.

Pius VI. "Verdammung und Verboth des Isenbiehlschen *Versuchs über die Weissagung vom Emmanuel*" [Condemnation and prohibition of Isenbiehl's *Essay on the Prophecy of Emmanuel*]. *Religions-Journal*, special edition. Mainz: Johann Joseph Alef: 1779. https://www.digitale-sammlungen.de/en/view/bsb11113530.

Pius IX. *Dei Filius*. Translated by Henry Edward Manning. https://www.ccel.org/ccel/schaff/creeds2.v.ii.i.html.

Pius XII. "Allocutio ad Patres Societatis Iesu in XXIX Congregatione generali electores" [Speech to the Fathers of the Society of Jesus at the 29th general congregation of electors]. *Acta Apostolicae Sedis* 38 (1946): 381–85.

Pohle, Joseph. *Lehrbuch der Dogmatik* [Textbook of dogmatics]. Vol. 1. Rev. ed. Michael Gierens. Paderborn: Schöningh, 1936.

Pollack, Detlef and Gergely Rosta. *Religion in der Moderne: Ein internationaler Vergleich* [Religion in modernity: An international comparison]. Frankfurt a. M.: Campus, 2015.

Pottmeyer, Hermann Josef. "Auf fehlbare Weise unfehlbar? Zu einer neuen Form päpstlichen Lehrens" [Fallibly infallible? On a new form of papal teaching]. *Stimmen der Zeit* 217 (1999): 233–42.

———. *Die Rolle des Papsttums im dritten Jahrtausend* [The role of the papacy in the third millennium]. Freiburg i. B.: Herder, 1999.

———. "Modernisierung in der katholischen Kirche am Beispiel der Kirchenkonzeption des I. und II. Vatikanischen Konzils" [Modernization in the Catholic Church using the example of the conception of church in the First and Second Vatican Councils]. In *Vatikanum II und Modernisierung. Historische, theologische und soziologische Perspektiven* [Vatican II and modernization: Historical, theological, and sociological perspectives], edited by Franz-Xaver Kaufmann and Arnold Zingerle, 131–46. Paderborn: Schöningh, 1996.

————. *Unfehlbarkeit und Souveränität: Die päpstliche Unfehl-barkeit im System der ultramontanen Ekklesiologie des 19. Jahrhunderts* [Infallibility and sovereignty: Papal infallibility within the system of nineteenth-century ultramontane ecclesiology]. Mainz: Grünewald, 1975.

Pröpper, Thomas. *Theologische Anthropologie* [Theological anthropology]. Vol. 2. Freiburg i. B.: Herder, 2011.

Quasten, Johannes, and Joseph C. Plumpe, eds. *The Epistles of St. Clement of Rome and St. Ignatius of Antioch*. Translated by James A. Kleist. New York: Paulist Press, 1946.

Rahner, Karl. "Naturwissenschaft und vernünftiger Glaube" [Natural science and reasonable faith]. In Karl Rahner, *Sämtliche Werke 30: Anstöße systematischer Theologie: Beiträge zur Fundamentaltheologie und Dogmatik* [Complete works, vol. 30: Impulses in systematic theology: Contributions to fundamental theology and dogmatics], 399–432. Freiburg i. B.: Herder, 2009.

————. "Was ist eine dogmatische Aussage?" [What is a dogmatic ruling?]. In Karl Rahner, *Sämtliche Werke 12: Menschsein und Menschwerdung Gottes: Studien zur Grundlegung der Dogmatik, der Christologie, Theologischen Anthropologie und Eschatologie* [Complete works 12: God's being human and becoming human: Studies on the foundations of dogmatics, Christology, theological anthropology, and eschatology], 150–70. Freiburg i. B.: Herder, 2005.

Ratzinger, Joseph. "Bemerkungen zum Schema 'De fontibus revelationis'" [Remarks on the schema "De fontibus revelationis"]. In Joseph Ratzinger, *Gesammelte Schriften 7/1: Zur Lehre des Zweiten Vatikanischen Konzils* [Collected writings 7/1: On the doctrine of the Second Vatican Council], 157–74. Freiburg i. B.: Herder, 2012.

————. "Stellungnahme" [Statement of Opinion]. *Stimmen der Zeit* 217 (1999): 169–71.

Reese-Schäfer, Walter. *Politische Theorie heute: Neuere Tendenzen und Entwicklungen* [Political theory today: More recent tendencies and developments]. Munich: De Gruyter, 2000.

Reiser, Marius. "Die Prinzipien der biblischen Hermeneutik und ihr Wandel unter dem Einfluss der Aufklärung" [The principles of biblical hermeneutics and its transformation under the influence of the Enlightenment]. In Marius Reiser, *Bibelkritik und Auslegung in der Heiligen Schrift: Beiträge zur Geschichte der biblischen Exegese und Hermeneutik* [Bible criticism and interpretation in the Holy Scriptures: Contributions to the history of biblical exegesis and hermeneutics], 219–76. Tübingen: Mohr Siebeck, 2007.

Rhonheimer, Martin. *Christentum und säkularer Staat: Geschichte—Gegenwart—Zukunft* [Christianity and the secular state: Past—present—future]. Freiburg i. B.: Herder, 2014.

Rohls, Jan. *Protestantische Theologie der Neuzeit, Bd. I: Die Voraussetzungen und das 19. Jahrhundert* [Protestant theology in the modern era, vol. 1: The preconditions and the 19th century]. Tübingen: Utb, 2018.

Sailer, Johann Michael. *Vernunftlehre für Menschen wie sie sind, d. i. Anleitung zur Erkenntniß und Liebe der Wahrheit. III. Band* [Theory of reason for people as they are, i. e. Instruction on insight and love of the truth. Vol. 3]. 2nd rev. ed. Munich: Johann Baptist Strobel, 1795. https://www.digitale-sammlungen.de/en/view/bsb10044283.

Salmann, Elmar. *Der geteilte Logos: Zum offenen Prozeß von neuzeitlichem Denken und Theologie* [The divided *logos*: On the open case of modern thought and theology]. Rome: Pontificio Ateneo S. Anselmo, 1992.

Saxer, Victor. "Die Organisation der nachapostolischen Gemeinden (70–180)" [The organization of postapostolic congregations (70–180)]. In *Die Geschichte des Christentums. Bd. I: Die Zeit des Anfangs* [The history of Christianity. Vol. 1: The early period], edited by Luce Pietri, 269–339. Freiburg i. B.: Herder, 2003.

Scarnecchia, D. Brian. *Bioethics, Law and Human Life Issues: A Catholic Perspective on Marriage, Family, Contraception, Abortion, Reproductive Technology, and Death and Dying.* Lanham, MD: Scarecrow, 2010.

Schatz, Klaus. *Vaticanum I: 1869–1870. Band 2: Von der Eröffnung bis zur Konstitution "Dei Filius"* [Vatican I: 1869–1870. Vol. 2: From the opening to the constitution "Dei Filius"]. Paderborn: Schöningh, 1993.

————. *Vaticanum I: 1869–1870. Band 3: Unfehlbarkeits-diskussion und Rezeption* [Vatican I: 1869–1870. Vol. 3: The discussion on infallibility and reception]. Paderborn: Schöningh, 1994.

Scheeben, Matthias Joseph. *Handbuch der Katholischen Dogmatik: Erstes Buch: Theologische Erkenntnislehre* [Handbook of Catholic dogmatics: First book; Theological epistemology], edited by Martin Grabmann. Freiburg i. B.: Herder, 1948.

Schimank, Uwe. *Die Entscheidungsgesellschaft: Komplexität und Rationalität der Moderne* [The decision society: Complexity and rationality of the modern era]. Wiesbaden: Verlag für Sozialwissenschaften, 2005.

Schmaus, Michael. *Katholische Dogmatik 4: Die Lehre von den Sakramenten* [Catholic dogmatics 4: Teachings on the sacraments]. Munich: Max Hueber, 1957.

Schmidt, Volker H. "Globale Moderne: Skizze eines Konzeptualisierungsversuchs" [Global modernity: Sketch of an attempted conceptualization]. In *Moderne und Religion: Kontroversen um Modernität und Säkularisierung* [Modernity and religion: Controversies surrounding modernity and secularization], edited by Ulrich Willems et al., 27–73. Bielefeld: transcript, 2013.

Schmied, Augustin. "'Schleichende Infallibilisierung': Zur Diskussion um das kirchliche Lehramt" ["Creeping infallibilization": On the discussion of the magisterium of the Church]. In *In Christus zum Leben befreit: Festschrift für Bernhard Häring* [In Christ, freed to live: *Festschrift* for Bernhard Häring], edited by Josef Römelt and Bruno Hidber, 250–74. Freiburg i. B.: Herder, 1992.

Schmiedl, Joachim. "Humanae vitae in der Diskussion der Würzburger Synode" [*Humanae vitae* in the discussions of the Würzburg Synod]. In Humanae vitae—*die anstößige Enzyklika: Eine kritische Würdigung* [*Humanae vitae*—the objectionable encyclical: A critical appraisal], edited by Konrad Hilpert and Sigrid Müller, 216–26. Freiburg i. B.: Herder, 2018.

Schnädelbach, Herbert. "Aufklärug und Religionskritik" [Enlightenment and criticism of religion]. In Herbert Schnädelbach,

Religion in der modernen Welt: Vorträge, Abhandlungen, Streitschriften [Religion in the modern world: Lectures, treatises, polemics], 11–34. Frankfurt a. M.: Fischer Taschenbuch, 2009.

———. "Gescheiterte Moderne?" [Failed modernity?]. In Herbert Schnädelbach, *Zur Rehabilitierung des* animal rationale*: Vorträge und Abhandlungen* [On the rehabilitation of the "rational animal": Lectures and treatises], 2:431–46. Frankfurt a. M.: Suhrkamp, 1992.

Scholder, Klaus. "Grundzüge der theologischen Aufklärung in Deutschland" [Basics of the theological Enlightenment in Germany]. In *Aufklärung, Absolutismus und Bürgertum in Deutschland* [Enlightenment, absolutism, and bourgeoisie in Germany], edited by Franklin Kopitzsch, 294–318. Munich: Nymphenburger, 1976.

Schreiber, Stefan. "Von der Verkündigung Jesu zum verkündigten Christus" [From the annunciation of Jesus to the proclaimed Christ]. In *Christologie* [Christology], edited by Karlheinz Ruhstorfer, 69–140. Paderborn: Utb, 2018.

Schubert, Anselm. "Wie die Reformation zu ihrem Namen kam" [How the Reformation got its name]. *Archiv für Reformationsgeschichte* 107 (2016): 343–54.

Schüller, Bruno. *Die Begründung sittlicher Urteile: Typren ethischer Argumentation in der Moraltheologie* [The justification of moral judgments: Types of ethical argumentation in moral theology]. Düsseldorf: Patmos, 1987.

Seewald, Michael. *Dogma im Wandel: Wie Glaubenslehren sich entwickeln* [Dogmas undergoing transformation: How doctrines of faith develop]. Freiburg i. B.: Herder, 2018.

———. "Religion als Kontingenzbewältigung? Präzisierungen zu einem gängigen Topos in Auseinandersetzung mit Niklas Luhmann, Hermann Lübbe und Ernst Tugendhat" [Religion as coping with contingency? Concretizing a common trope through engagement with Niklas Luhmann, Hermann Lübbe, and Ernst Tugendhat]. *Jahrbuch für Religionsphilosophie* 15 (2016): 152–79.

———. "Religiöse Überlieferungen im Zeitalter des 'häretischen Imperativs': Krisenempfindung und Aufbrüche kirchlicher Traditionsdeutung" [Religious transmissions in the age of the 'heretical imperative': Feelings of crisis and new paths in ecclesiastical interpretation of tradition]. In *Kirche ohne Jugend: Ist die Glaubensweitergabe am Ende?* [Church without youth: Is the transmission of faith at an end?], edited by Clauß Peter Sajak, Michael Langer, 45–69. Freiburg i. B.: Herder, 2018.

———. "Sakramententheologie—mit einem oder mit zwei Augen? Eine (nicht nur) dogmatische Nachlese zum Kommunionstreit" [Sacramental theology—with one eye or two? A (not just) dogmatic investigation into the debate over Communion]. In *Eucharistie—Kirche—Ökumene: Aspekte und Hintergründe des Kommunionstreits* [Eucharist—Church—ecumenicalism: Aspects and backgrounds on the debate over communion], edited by Thomas Söding, Wolfgang Thönissen, 172–88. Freiburg i. B.: Herder, 2019.

———. *Theologie aus anthropologischer Ansicht: Der Entwurf Franz Oberthürs (1745–1831) als Beitrag zum dogmatischen Profil der Katholischen Aufklärung* [Theology from an anthropological perspective: Franz Oberthür's (1745–1831) suggestion as a contribution to the Catholic Enlightenment's dogmatic profile]. Innsbruck: Tyrolia, 2016.

———. "Worüber wird gestritten, wenn Glaubenslehren sich entwickeln? Ein kontingenztheoretischer Vorschlag" [What is being debated when doctrines develop? A proposal from the point of view of contingency theory]. *Münchener Theologische Zeitschrift* 69 (2018): 279–87.

Shuve, Karl. "Cyprian of Carthage's writings from the rebaptism controversy: Two revisionary proposals reconsidered." *Journal of Theological Studies* 61, no. 2 (2010): 627–43.

Sieben, Hermann Josef. *Kleines Lexikon zur Geschichte der Konzilsidee* [Brief encyclopedia on the concept of the Council]. Paderborn: Schöningh, 2018.

———. *Studien zum Ökumenischen Konzil: Definitionen und Begriffe, Tagebücher und Augustinus-Rezeption (Konziliengeschichte B: Untersuchungen)* [Studies on the ecumenical council: Definitions and terms, diaries, and Augustine scholarship (Council History B: Research)]. Paderborn: Schöningh, 2010.

Siebenrock, Roman A. "'Zeichen der Zeit': Zur Operationalisierung des christlichen Bekenntnisses vom universalen Heilswillen Gottes" ["Signs of the times": On the operationalization of the Christian profession for God's universal salvific will]. *Zeitschrift für Katholische Theologie* 136 (2014): 46–63.

Spörl, Johannes. "Das Alte und das Neue im Mittelalter: Studien zum Problem des mittelalterlichen Fortschrittsbewußtseins" [The old and the new in the Middle Ages: Studies on the problem of a medieval awareness of progress]. *Historisches Jahrbuch* 50 (1930): 297–341.

Stark, Rodney. "Secularization R.I.P." *Journal for the Scientific Study of Religion* 90 (1999): 249–73.

Stollberg-Rillinger, Barbara. "Cultures of Decision-Making" (German Historical Institute, Annual Lecture 2015), London 2015.

———. "Was heißt Ideengeschichte?" [What does "history of ideas" mean?]. In *Ideengeschichte* [History of ideas], edited by Barbara Stollberg-Rilinger, 7–42. Stuttgart: Franz Steiner, 2010.

Striet, Magnus. *Ernstfall Freiheit: Arbeiten an der Schleifung der Bastionen* [The hard case of freedom: Working to raze the fortresses]. Freiburg i. B.: Herder, 2018.

Stubenrauch, Bertram. *Dialogisches Dogma: Der christliche Auftrag zur interreligiösen Begegnung* [Dialogical dogma: The Christian task of interreligious encounter]. Freiburg i. B.: Herder, 1995.

Tertullian. "Ad Scapulam." Translated by S. Thelwall. In *The Writings of Quintus Sept. Flor. Tertullianus*. Vol. 1. Edinburgh: T. & T. Clark, 1869. In *Ante-Nicene Christian Library: Translations of the Writings of the Fathers Down to A.D. 325,* edited by Alexander Roberts and James Donaldson. Edinburgh: T. & T. Clark, 1869.

Theobald, Christoph. "Le développement de la notion des 'Vérités historiquement et logiquement connexes avec la Révélation'" [The development of the idea of "Truths historically and logically linked to the revelation"]. *Cristianesimo nella storia* 21 (2000): 37–70.

Theobald, Michael. *Das Evangelium nach Johannes: Kapitel 1–12* [The Gospel according to John: Chapters 1–12]. Regensburg: Friedrich Pustet, 2009.

Tück, Jan-Heiner. "Von der Zitadelle zur offenen Stadt: Geschichtliche Selbstvergewisserung und dialogische Öffnung auf dem Zweiten Vatikanum" [From citadel to open city: Historical self-assurance and dialogical opening in the Second Vatican Council]. In *Zukunft aus der Geschichte Gottes: Theologie im Dienst an einer Kirche für morgen: Für Peter Hünermann* [Future from the past of God: Theology in the service of a Church of tomorrow; For Peter Hünermann], edited by Guido Bausenhart, Margit Eckholt, and Linus Hauser, 144–69. Freiburg i. B.: Herder, 2014.

Unterburger, Klaus. "Internationalisierung von oben, oder: Schleiermacher, Humboldt und Harnack für die katholische Weltkirche? Das päpstliche Lehramt und die katholischen Fakultäten und Universitäten im 20. Jahrhundert" [Internationalization from above, or: Schleiermacher, Humboldt, and Harnack for a Catholic world church? The papal magisterium and the Catholic seminaries and universities in the twentieth century]. In *Transnationale Dimensionen wissenschaftlicher Theologie* [Transnational dimensions of scientific theology], edited by Claus Arnold and Johannes Wischmeyer, 53–68. Göttingen: Vandenhoeck & Ruprecht, 2013.

———. "'Reform der ganzen Kirche': Konturen, Ursachen und Wirkungen einer Leitidee und Zwangsvorstellung im Spätmittelalter" ['Reform of the entire Church': Outlines, causes, and effects of a late medieval guiding idea and obsession]. In *Reformen in der Kirche: Historische Perspektiven* [Reforms in the Church: Historical perspective], edited by Andreas Merkt, Günther Wassilowsky, and Gregor Wurst, 109–37. Freiburg i. B.: Herder, 2014.

Vacant, Jean-Michel-Alfred. *Le magistère ordinaire de l'Eglise et ses organes* [The ordinary magisterium and its bodies]. Paris: Delhommes et Briguet, 1887.

Wagner, Jochen. *Die Anfänge des Amtes in der Kirche: Presbyter und Episkopen in der frühchristlichen Literatur* [The beginnings of offices in the Church: Presbyters and bishops in early Christian writings]. Tübingen: Narr, 2011.

Wenz, Gunther. "Pannenbergs Kreis: Genese und erste Kritik eines theologischen Programms" [The Pannenberg circle: Development and initial assessment of a theological program]. In *Offenbarung als Geschichte: Implikationen und Konsequenzen eines theologischen Programms* [Revelation as history: implications and consequences of a theological program], edited by Gunter Wenz, 17–58. Göttingen: Vandenhoeck & Ruprecht, 2018.

Werbick, Jürgen. *Einführung in die theologische Wissenschaftslehre* [Introduction to the science of theology]. Freiburg i. B.: Herder, 2010.

Wolf, Hubert. *Johann Michael Sailer: Das postume Inquisitionsverfahren* [Johann Michael Sailer: The posthumous inquisition proceedings]. Paderborn: Schöningh, 2002.

———. "'Wahr ist, was gelehrt wird' statt 'Gelehrt wird, was wahr ist'? Zur Erfindung des ordentlichen Lehramts" ["What is taught is true" rather than "What is true is taught"? On the invention of the ordinary magisterium.]. In *Neutestamentliche Ämtermodelle im Kontext* [Contextualizing New Testament models of office], edited by Thomas Schmeller, Martin Ebner, and Rudolf Hoppe, 236–59. Freiburg i. B.: Herder, 2010.

Wolgast, Eike. "Politisches Kalkül und religiöse Entscheidung im Konfessionszeitalter" [Political calculus and religious decisions in the age of religious denominations]. *Luther* 76 (2005): 66–79.

———. "Reform/Reformation" [Reform/Reformation]. In Otto Brunner, Werner Conze, and Reinhart Koselleck (eds.). *Geschichtliche Grundbegriffe: Historisches Lexikon zur politisch-sozialen Sprache in Deutschland* [Basic historical terms: A historical lexicon of sociopolitical speech in Germany]. 5:313–60. Stuttgart: Klett-Cotta, 2004.